HEROES
of HOPE

Intimate Conversations with Six Abolitionists
and the Sex Trafficking Survivors They Serve

by David Trotter

Awaken Media

HEROES OF HOPE: Intimate Conversations with Six Abolitionists and the Sex Trafficking Survivors They Serve
by David Trotter

Designed by 8TRACKstudios - www.8trackstudios.com

ISBN: 978-1-935798-10-1

Dedicated to the "heroes of hope"
who invest more than anyone
could ever imagine as
they fight to end
sex trafficking
in our world.

Jeanne Allert
Bobbie Mark
Louise Allison
Jenny Williamson
Deena Graves
Stacia Freeman

I admire who you are.

TABLE OF CONTENTS

WE ALL NEED HOPE.

An Introduction to My Conversations

As our Chinese hosts led us from the hotel restaurant, down the elevator, and through a maze of hallways, my eyes adjusted to the neon lights that guided my steps through a corridor of private karaoke rooms. My mind was searching for some level of familiarity, but nothing could be found.

Walking through the door, I stepped into an area the size of an average American living room. Three walls were lined with built-in, wrap-around couches, and the fourth wall was a large screen with a short stage in front of it. Drinks were served, and our hosts picked out their favorite songs.

Frankly, I'm not much for booze *or* karaoke - especially when all the songs are in Mandarin, but nothing could have prepared me for what happened next. I was in China on a business trip to visit a manufacturing plant for a product my company was creating, but I got an education that extended beyond textiles.

A man in a suit walked through the door of our karaoke suite and led a group of 20 or so girls onto the stage - all dressed in traditional Chinese outfits and looking quite beautiful. While I'm not sure of their ages, most appeared to be older teens or 20-somethings, and they were smiling broadly at all of us. I was absolutely perplexed by what was going on.

Why are these girls standing in front of us?
Are they here to teach us karaoke?
Are they here to serve drinks?

"Which one would you like?" the man asked with a heavy accent.

"Huh? What do you mean?" I asked.

"Which one of these ladies do you want to be with?" he explained.

"Uhhhh...I'm good. I don't need any company tonight. I'm okay."

Call me naive, but I had no clue what was going on. I didn't want to offend my hosts, but I was extremely uncomfortable with the situation.

"Ah. I see...you must want a boy?" the man said as the room filled with laughter.

"No...no...I'm really okay," I re-assured them as I sunk lower into the couch. Thankfully, I was seated next to a 50-something businesswoman who I had been discussing manufacturing with, and I was able to continue the conversation.

Meanwhile, other men in the room made their choices and began to cozy up to the ladies as karaoke songs were sung. After awhile, I was able to politely excuse myself and head back to my room - all the while left wondering what would happen later in the evening with each of those girls.

Although I don't know the working conditions or expectations for those girls, I can only imagine that it was *not* limited to hanging out in that karaoke suite. While my experience in China may have been more subtle, I saw firsthand the blatant selling of ladies in both Thailand and India on separate trips, and my mind was stretched to capacity when I heard that children and women were being sold for sex in the United States.

What? In the United States?!?!

At some point, you probably had that experience as well.
Or, maybe you're coming to grips with that reality right now.

For years, I thought prostitutes just wanted to sell themselves. I thought sex trafficking was about foreign women brought into the U.S. I thought sex trafficking was like the movie *Taken* where a girl is kidnapped.

After my first documentary on orphans in India (*Mother India: Life Through the Eyes of the Orphan*), I started doing some research on sex trafficking in the United States, and my eyes were opened to what was happening "in plain sight."

- Over 80% percent of victims in confirmed sex trafficking cases were identified as U.S. citizens.[1]

- The average age a teen enters the sex trade in the U.S. is 12 to 14-year-old, and many victims are runaway girls who were sexually abused as children.[2]

- And, 100,000-300,000 American children are at risk of being trafficked for commercial sex each year.[3]

The US Government defines sex trafficking as "a commercial sex act induced by force, fraud, or coercion, or in which the person induced to perform such act has not attained 18 years of age."

Any minor engaged in a commercial sex act is considered a trafficking victim regardless of whether force, fraud, or coercion is involved. In other words, there is no such thing as a child prostitute. He or she is a trafficking victim.

While the image of a pimp and prostitute have been glamorized through movies such as *Pretty Woman* and *Hustle & Flow*, there is nothing beautiful about the dark underbelly of the sex industry.

These children and women don't *want* to be sold for sex.

"I think society as a whole needs to look at prostitution differently. There is no girl who grows up wanting to become a prostitute. It's just not like that," said Louise Allison, a survivor of sex trafficking and founder of Partners Against Trafficking Humans based in Little Rock, Arkansas.

---

1 http://www.bjs.gov/content/pub/press/cshti0810pr.cfm
2 http://aspe.hhs.gov/hsp/07/humantrafficking/litrev/
3 National Center for Missing and Exploited Children

"And, we really didn't play with hooker Barbies when we were kids and say that's exactly what I want to be when I grow up. No, we wanted to be nurses or stewardesses or something else. Don't drive by prostitutes and look down at them and call them names and be hateful to them - but love them, pray for them. Everybody can help in some way whether it's through prayer, financial support, volunteering. Everyone can help in some way."

By now, you're aware of the term **sex trafficking**.

To me, it's simply a politically-correct way of saying **sexual slavery**.

While public slavery in the United States is over, there is still a large market for buying and selling women and children…in your city. They are being sold through ads in the back weekly newspapers, posts on Backpage.com, at massage parlors, via escort services, at truck stops, and at a motel you drive by on a daily basis.

When I became aware of this fact, I couldn't stand by and *not* do something. As a filmmaker, I started watching documentaries on sex trafficking, but I found most of them to be completely depressing, and many were overly sexualized. I started to wonder if it was possible to produce a documentary that wasn't titillating, but was informative and full of hope.

After a positive experience with the distributor of my first film, I re-approached Word Entertainment about the possibility of a project of this type, and they were incredibly receptive. Through a relationship with Hope for Justice and Natalie Grant, I had the opportunity to meet and develop a friendship with the six female abolitionists profiled in this book.

The interviews you are about to read were conducted over the course of five months in Nashville, Baltimore, Sacramento, Little Rock, Houston, and Dallas during the filming of *IN PLAIN SIGHT: Stories of Hope and Freedom*. There's no way that we could possibly include all of this content into a film, but a book is a great medium to share these intimate interviews with a wide audience.

Not only have I included the interviews with the six abolitionists, but I wanted you to read the words of the brave survivors who I have had the privilege of interviewing for this project. Words can not fully describe the experience I had sitting down face to face with these survivors as they shared part of their life story with me. What an incredible privilege to have a small glimpse into what they've experienced and how they're healing.

More than anything, these women offer hope.

Without hope, we'll be paralyzed by depression and believe there's nothing we can do. That's why their stories are so important. When we hear how an ordinary person - just like you and me - became aware of the issue of sex trafficking and chose to do something extraordinary about it, we can be motivated to take action. When we read the words of a young woman who has been ravaged for the profit and pleasure of others but is now finding hope and healing at an aftercare home, we can have hope for the victims who are yet to be rescued.

Hope is a currency that we can't afford to live without.

That's why I call all these women "Heroes of Hope." They are my heroes - either for leveraging their lives for the sake of victims or surviving abuse and courageously seeking restoration and healing. In both cases, I'm given hope for the eradication of sex trafficking in our nation.

A few things you should know about the survivor interviews...

- Each survivor was given the opportunity to share her story by the founder of the aftercare home where she were staying or affiliated.

- No minors were interviewed for the film.

- The survivor's therapist was required to state that the individual was "fit" to be interviewed so that our conversation would not harm her in any way.

- A staff member of the aftercare home was present during the interview at all times, and the survivor was able to decline to comment on any question during the process.

- Each survivor was filmed in a way that she felt comfortable - either full face, partial face, or silhouette. Photographs included in this book are screen stills taken from the documentary.

- Each survivor was offered further counseling after the interview if something had been triggered by the experience.

- Some names have been changed to protect survivors.

- These questions were asked initially to guide the person through the process of telling their story for the sake of the documentary - not originally designed for a printed version.

- The interviews have been edited for readability, but I sought to maintain the "voice" of the individual being interviewed.

To begin, I have included a conversation with my co-executive producer and narrator of *IN PLAIN SIGHT*, Natalie Grant. She is a Grammy nominated, five time Gospel Music Association Dove Award winner for Female Vocalist of the Year, and she is the co-founder of Hope for Justice. Her passion to end sex trafficking in our world is unending, and I want you to hear why she is committed to this cause.

Let's go ahead and listen in...

David Trotter
December 2014

NATALIE GRANT

Co-founder of Hope for Justice

After seeing human trafficking portrayed on a favorite television show, Natalie and her husband boarded a plane to India and witnessed the travesty firsthand. While her heart was broken for the young lives being ravaged by sex trafficking overseas, she was even more shocked to find out that it was happening in her own city - even near where her family lived.

The reality of the global issue of human trafficking led her to start an organization in 2006 and recently collaborated to co-found Hope for Justice. While Natalie continues to travel and perform as a highly-acclaimed singer and songwriter, she uses her platform to educate audiences about the issue and motivate them to take action.

DT: Why is sex trafficking such an important issue for you?

Natalie: We're talking about the most innocent among us. I think this issue is so important and imperative, because once you learn about it and you learn the truth about it, not as just some idea you saw on television, but you learn that the reality is there are children who are being ravaged day in and day out, if you have a heart beating on the inside of you, I don't understand how it couldn't be important to you. We are talking about the most innocent among us. I became passionate about this issue before I ever became a mother, but now that I'm a mother, I mean you can bet that it has only deepened my passion.

DT: When did you first begin to hear about this issue?

Natalie: The first time I heard about it I was home from a day off of touring, and I was chilling out. My family and I are watching my favorite television show, which is Law & Order: Special Victims Unit. And, you know, they always say that Law & Order is ripped from the headlines, so it's loosely based on fact.

I remember they were depicting children being sold out of the back of a van in New York City, and I'm not trying to be sarcastic about such a serious topic, but I've bought handbags – knockoff handbags – out of the back of a van in New York City, but I'd never seen children for sale. It was almost irritating to me, because I thought what are you trying – I mean you're trying to make me believe that kids are being sold, you know, in New York? There's no way.

This was several years ago before everybody started talking about human trafficking. There's just something that happened inside of me as I continued to watch the episode, and I think I just started saying, "What if...what if this is real?"

The episode ended and I went to Google, and I literally punched into Google "what is human trafficking" and that's the first time that all the statistics started to pop up - more slaves in the world today than in any other point in our history, most of them under the age of 18 and the high percentage of them who are sex trafficking victims. From there, it led me to look up faith-based organizations that fight human trafficking, and three months later my husband and I were on the plane flying across the world and stepped off that plane in Mumbai, India walked straight in the red light district, toured a brothel and saw five-year olds for sale, and it just it has wrecked me for life.

DT: Obviously, you've seen this internationally, but what was your reaction when you began to learn that this was happening in the U.S.?

Natalie: You know it was one thing to know that this was happening in India, and that was really the place where my eyes were opened to it and I saw real human beings for sale. Then, you come back home and as a singer, I'm thinking, "I'm going to tell everybody I know about this" - but sometimes it's almost easier to believe it when it's happening to somebody that looks nothing like you, doesn't speak your same language, and seems like they're in a very far off place.

When you start talking about your neighborhood, your town, all of a sudden you no longer have to go across the world, but literally across the street. For me, I was watching the local news report, and they were reporting in Nashville where I live that twelve girls under the age of eighteen were found in the same apartment with just dirty mattresses on the floor. They had broken up this brothel, and it was one mile from my front door.

It did something different to me at that point, and it's not that these children are any more important than the children in India, it's just that these children are in my town. And, how is it that I know nothing about this? And right here – right around the corner from my house this is happening.

DT: When you started talking to people about this issue, what was their reaction?

Natalie: When I very first started talking about it, it was before it was being really talked about on television and on the news and people raising awareness about it. So, people just didn't believe it was true. They just thought, no, and you get into an argument about prostitution versus trafficking and well, "these people chose this for themselves." And, you try to explain, "No, no, they didn't." And, even if this is a sixteen-year old runaway, how could she really choose this for her life?

When I was sixteen years old and I wanted to get my ears pierced, I had to get a permission slip from my parents. I had to get a consent form signed by my parents, because it was deemed that I was not responsible enough to be able to make the decision to get my ears pierced.

Well, if you're a sixteen-year old girl, how are you deemed responsible enough to choose to prostitute yourself? It doesn't even make any sense. These girls are being exploited, and it doesn't matter their background or where they come from or how they even got into it, it doesn't change the fact that they need to be rescued.

When I started to talk to people about it, the first thing was disbelief, the second thing was, "Okay, maybe I'll start to believe that it's happening very far away from me, but there's no way you're going to convinced me that it's happening in Des Moines, Iowa." I think that the awareness that's been happening over the last few years has really helped to open people's eyes to the truth of the fact that it is happening and not only is it happening, but it's growing at an alarming rate.

DT: Why did you start an organization focused on this issue?

Natalie: When I came back from India and I started thinking about working with organizations that are established and were well-known organizations that I know and love, I couldn't find one that was specifically geared towards addressing quality restorative care in the US. Because the issue was still on the back burner, people weren't even aware of it really happening in the way that it does, it just wasn't at the forefront. I wanted a way that I knew that the support we raised and what we did would specifically help these victims, and I wanted it to specifically help in the restoration piece.

I'm not the police, I'm not going to go in and arrest the bad guys and do a raid. I'm not a lawyer, and I'm not going to be able to prosecute them, but I am a Christian and a member of the church at large. I felt like as a person of faith that it was our job to be on the frontlines of restoration. When I started to really learn about this issue and about the lack of the restoration piece, I said, "Okay, we've got people getting the bad guys, but when we rescue victims, they're just being put in juvenile detention. They're being treated like a criminal." We've got to do something about this.

Because they need them to testify against their perpetrator, that's when I realized something must be done to offer quality restoration and not just throwing a shelter together. These are specific victims with specific needs that have to be met through trained qualified professionals who can treat their physical needs, their spiritual needs, and their medical needs. And, then give them just a chance at wholeness. They're so broken - broken in ways we can't even imagine, but there is an opportunity to help put those broken pieces back together.

DT: What are some of the positive things that you're seeing happen nationwide?

Natalie: Some of the most positive things about this - and this is a very dark issue - it's just very difficult to find hope until you meet the victims who've come out and have had the opportunity to be restored. Seeing what hope does - hope is the promise that a better day is coming. And, to see that some of these victims who have more reason than anyone to have no hope. To see that hope restored in their lives through the work of Hope for Justice has been incredible.

I think one of the most incredible things that's happened is just more people know about it, more people are aware that it's happening, more people in powerful positions are aware. In 2013, we heard the President of the United States for the first time call this "modern day slavery". We see the FBI taking note and rising up and putting task forces together that are going in and doing raids and getting children out by the dozens.

We have to continue to do the work so that those who are rescued have a place to be restored. Now that more people are aware, they are realizing the desperate need of offering restoration to those that are rescued.

DT: As you think about the IN PLAIN SIGHT documentary and benefit album, why have you chosen to get involved?

Natalie: This was a very easy decision for me, because it's taking creative arts and allowing people to learn about trafficking through that medium. To me, there's nothing more powerful. Especially for me since I'm a visual learner, so when I see something, I digest it better.

To know that this issue, you can talk about it and talk about it and talk about it, but when you give people the opportunity to see something on a screen, I think it does a better job of cutting straight to the heart and letting them learn the facts, learn the truth, and have a way of giving them an opportunity to be involved. I think that it's going to do a great job of telling the truth and letting people see the reality of sex trafficking in the United States of America and a way that they can be involved.

Then, to have a companion music piece, I mean as a musical creative person, I don't think there's any way to get to somebody's heart better than through music. Especially with a topic like this, it is so heavy and so dark that the music will help be a soothing balm to people's hearts who are going to be wrecked by this issue. And, I say that's what happened to me. I was wrecked for life, and once you learned the truth, it wrecks you.

DT: As you think about IN PLAIN SIGHT, what are your hopes for this project?

Natalie: My hope for this project is that a lot more people would become aware of the issue in the United States. I think that the way this film tells that story will do a fantastic job of educating, and you have to start there. You have to start with opening people's eyes to it, educating them, and raising awareness.

But then, I think it's also going to lead people to a place where they can do something with this new found awareness. A lot of times we become aware, but awareness without action just leads to nothing.

I also feel like this is such a hot topic of the moment that now is the time ,because now is the time that people's eyes and ears are more keen to hearing this truth than ever before, and we have to pounce on that opportunity. And so, instead of seeing an increase in human trafficking, we will see a decrease in it.

But also, I feel like what it will do is give people the opportunity to invest in long term recovery and not just in short term awareness. We can wear a bracelet and a t-shirt and be an abolitionist, but that it's actually something that's real that is doing something to put those broken pieces for those victims back together again.

DT: As you think about the fact that you're a mother of three young daughters, what is your hope for the world they are going to be living in - in the next ten, fifteen, twenty, forty years, sixty years after you're gone? What is your hope for them and their life in regard to this issue?

Natalie: My hope for my daughters is that when they are grown they will live in a world without this. When you hear the numbers and the staggering statistics, it's hard sometimes to believe that could be a reality. But I imagine when Martin Luther King gave his speech on the fact that he had a dream that he might have had many days when he never thought that dream will become a reality.

To watch the abolishment of that kind of slavery, but then to know that we're now living in a day and age where slavery still exists. My prayer would be that my kids, when they are grown, would look back and see, "Look at what our mom was involved in. Look at what she did to not just live her life in the safe little box, but that she got out of her box and stood up for the things that matter."

This is one of the reasons that I do what I do with my music and that I do what I do with my platform. I have to be away from my children a lot, and there are many times when I want to quit and throw in the towel and just stay home, but I have daughters who are looking to me to set an example of what it looks like to be a strong woman who stands for the things that matter, the things that are important, to fight for those things that will last forever. And, I want my daughters to see a mom who did that so they can live in a world without human trafficking.

Hope for Justice
Nashville, TN
www.hopeforjustice.org

Hope for Justice identifies and rescues victims, advocates on their behalf, provides restorative care which rebuilds lives and trains frontline professionals to tackle slavery.

JEANNE ALLERT

Founder of The Samaritan Women
Baltimore, MD

After owning and managing a successful consulting practice focused the use of Internet technologies, Jeanne Allert came face to face - literally - with the issue of sex trafficking in her city. With more passion than actual plan, she purchased a 23-acre dilapidated estate in Baltimore and transformed it into The Samaritan Women (founded in 2007) with the help of local volunteers. After walking away from her business, Jeanne now focuses completely on the restoration of victims of sex trafficking.

Jeanne is a compelling speaker on the topic of domestic human trafficking and has delivered awareness presentations in several states. She is a member of the Department of Homeland Security Blue Campaign and graduate of the FBI Citizen's Academy.

DT: Tell me what life was like for Jeanne Allert before you became aware of sex trafficking. What were you all about? What were you doing? What was life all about for you?

Jeanne: You know it's hard to say...it's almost embarrassing to say what life was like, because I grew up in a very lovely, middle-class, Midwestern family with an intact family life and parents. We had the great privilege of traveling as a young family, and I spent most of my years overseas. With 60's parents who empowered their daughter to be anything that she could be, you're going to go to college and you're going to, of course have your own career. That was very much pumped into me, and I responded to that.

And so, I did all of the things that we say in America you're supposed to want to do: the education, the job, traveling, having a family, having your own money...all those things and continued to do them with the degree of excellence.

And, long about forty, I think I hit my wall, and now I call it my "wall of affluence", because I had the privilege of working in the Internet space and made really good money and lived very comfortably. I don't begrudge any of that, because now I see why it had value. At the time I realized I had everything externally that you're supposed to want, yet the inside was really empty.

I went into this dark night of the soul that lasted about four years of just sort of wandering around and wondering about what's the point. It's interesting now, because I encounter a lot of people who are going through that same wandering and looking for a purpose. During that period of time, I found myself pursuing some rather odd quests - not the least of which was going to seminary. I wasn't raised in a terribly religious household, but I was looking for answers and so that was one place to look.

Then, I got connected with a group that was doing outreach to women in prostitution on the streets of Baltimore and honestly my answer was, "Sure, why not?" So, I bumbled into that. Little did I know, that was all a Divine appointment to put me at a particular place in time where I was going to encounter faces and names and lives that up unto this point, frankly, I don't even think I saw them. I think that they sort of hovered under my gaze of achievement, and so there was this whole forgotten class of people in my life.

So, I'm sitting there on the stoop with this girl, and she's telling me about how she's a mother...and I'm a mother. And, she's telling me about how she had all these dreams and aspirations when she was a child, and I can remember that. And, she talked about her family, and I have good memories of my family. And, the point is the more we talk, the more I realized that the gap between us just got smaller and smaller...until frankly I went home that night thinking I would just erase this out of my mind and go, "Well, that was interesting."

I'm washing the dishes, and all of a sudden, it's just as if my whole soul just collapsed. I fell to the floor and started bawling, and I cried for probably a good three hours. I remember my daughter coming up to me and saying, "I am never going to let you go out there again because it's too hard. It's too hard on you."

I had one of those moments where I think I just spoke what was in my heart, and I turned to her and I said, "It's because of this brokenness that I have to go again." And, that's kind of what started it.

I realized that my heart was finally broken for something, and that began an incredible fast forward in my life that took about two months to unfold which resulted in my buying a 23-acre estate in Baltimore giving up my company, walking away from that profession that I'd had for fifteen years.

I even told my daughter, "You might not got to college, honey, because mom is giving it all up, and we're going all in." And, she was really cool and said, "You know mom, I know why you're doing this and so it's okay and I'm with you."

I then started trying to find out who's going to help these women, because when I was down there on the streets with them, I kept having that nag in my heart that kept saying, "Somebody should do something. Somebody should be doing something to help these ladies." That's when you realize you walk smack into a mirror and that maybe that somebody is you, and it was for me.

I began to learn about the issue of prostitution and as I dovetailed that with the lives and stories of these women, I realized that there wasn't anybody I had encountered who was there by choice. There wasn't a single woman who said, "This was my goal for my life." That girl who is now estranged from her children and on heroin and just needs enough money to find a place to sleep tonight, that was never her dream or her aspiration, and yet, here she was. We drive by her, and I probably at some point in my life was that person who drove by in my fancy car, and didn't see her.

The more I learned about human trafficking and the more I realized that these individuals are victims. They are victims not only of the crime itself, but they are victims very often of an entire trajectory of issues - whether it's being molested in the home as a child, whether it's being turned out by a toxic family member, whether it is being a throwaway child.

These kids are just doing what any kid would do which is look for connection and look for family and look for relationship and look for somebody that's going to love them. It is only natural to assume when you are out there just unfettered looking for love, the first one who's going to find you is somebody who's offering it with the wrong kind of intention.

As we look at the issue of human trafficking, we have to look not just at this through the lens of a criminal act, but this is a greater statement of what's going on in society and how are we treating people. There are four and five-year olds who are being sexually abused in the home, and nobody's talking about it. And, they don't have any place that's safe for them to report it.

To the woman who is trying to go to college, and she's being told, well, here is how you can make some money to pay for tuition or pay for books. She feels like, "I'm trying to better myself, I don't have anything, I'm trying to have something, so I can do this, right?" What she doesn't realize is, no, what it's going to do is set you on a whole different path.

Or, to the people who are compromised by poverty or by a set of other factors whether it's language, ethnicity, a sense of limited choices, generational prostitution. There are systemic issues that culminate in the issue of human trafficking, and that's where my learning has taken me up to this point.

DT: Talk to me specifically about the moment when you went with the group from church down to connect with some ladies on the street. Talk me through that whole scene. You walk up, what are you feeling when you're walking up on the street for the first time and sitting down with the girl on the stoop? What was that conversation like?

Jeanne: It was in August, and it was hot. It's one of those days where the pavement has steam coming up. We were a crazy bunch of church people, definitely going after forgiveness, not permission, and we wanted to bring just some joy into this bleak part of the city.

We had conspired for a few weeks to create an experience, and we're literally blocking off a street without permission. We're schlepping in a moon bounce, face painting, hot dogs, cotton candy, clothing donations, and school supplies. You name it...whether it was giveaways or whether it was just fun things we could do. We wanted to engage with the kids, and we wanted to connect with the parents.

We had it set up so there were going to be people in all of these different areas. It was one of those great days where it really worked out well, because everybody was hot, so they were kind of coming out to see what the commotion was.

I remember I was standing on Payson Street near the corner by the moon bounce and the hot dog stand, and I looked across the street. There was this waif of a girl, and she was walking towards the corner, not in a straight line. She kind of wavered...tiny little thing. There was just something about her that just emoted a desperation, a need, and I don't know what possessed me. I just got up and made a beeline and walked over to her, and as I'm walking there I'm thinking, "This is really going to be threatening to her." She's got this personal chaos going on, and this person just comes right up in her face, but I did it anyway.

I remember I just walked right up to her and I said, "Honey, are you okay? Can I get you anything?" And, she said she was thirsty. And I said, "Well, that's great, because I'd love to get you something to drink and something to eat and why don't you come join us." And so, she came across the street with me, we sat on the stoop, and I remember she – she was wasted. She was – it's really hard to describe how – it was almost like watching a bit of a horror movie. Her eyes would roll back in her head, and I remember looking at her lips are all chapped, and she had sores on her arms, on her legs. It's that moment where you just think, "Am I in a third world country?"

I sent somebody out to go get her a frosty, because you know the soda wasn't good enough..."Go get her whatever she wants." We found some ice cubes, and I remember she was rubbing her lips with the ice cubes. Then, when we came with the drink, perhaps one of the moments that really broke my heart was, I handed her the drink with the straw coming out, and she was so high that she couldn't find the hole. You know she just kept poking herself in the face, and yet, she could carry on this conversation, and then she'd drift out.

I remember at one moment I'm literally taking the straw and putting it in her mouth, and she responded to it almost like an infant would. It's crushing me inside, because I was mad at the drugs, I was mad at her circumstance, I was mad at the fact that somebody could get to this place and everything in me was bringing out this fierce protection.

We got her something to eat and she would occasionally drift into this lucidity, and she talked about her life and where she was from. She talked about how she just comes into the city to work, but she doesn't live here. We both knew what she was talking about, and it went on for maybe a couple of hours. She would occasionally, you know, just sort of fall out, and then she'd come back. I didn't really know what to do with her except just be present.

Then, my colleagues were all packed up, you know, the moon bounce was deflated, and everything was in the truck, and we were all getting ready to go. One of the guys on our team is like, "Jeanne, come on we've got to go. We've got to go." By then, I knew her name was Heather. I knew where she was from, and I had just created such – I just felt such a connection to her. I remember I turned to him like I had probably spun on my shoulders and I said, "I'm not leaving her." [laughs] My colleagues were probably like, "Oh, dear, what's happened?"

It's because two lives had connected. And, to this day, Heather will always be that girl who is the face and the name in my heart, and I believe that sometimes that's what God does in our lives is make something real for you. That's what had to happen for me is...I had to meet Heather, and I had to realize this problem is real, and it has a pulse and it desperately, desperately needs help.

DT: What was your next step with her after that encounter? How did you follow up or connect?

Jeanne: You know what's so frustrating about doing street outreach is you get a moment, and you just have to hope that it was a seed well planted. It's like drive-by relationships. I had given our contact information, but the ball was in her court. I knew that I might not ever see her again, but I think I became a stalker in the neighborhood. [laughs] Of course, every weekend we're down there, I've always got one eye out. You know, we're still there ministering to the other girls, but I'm always looking, right?

I'm always looking for that little blonde, and we would talk to other girls and I'm like, "Hey, do you know anybody named Heather?" Well, here's the problem, you know, there are about five names that get recycled down on the street, and you're either a Britney or a Star or a Heather or a Katie or something like that, and you never know if it's her.

A few months later, one of my colleagues said she had seen her. Of course, I made a beeline to go back down there and caught her coming out of this restaurant. We got her back to our outreach house, and I just want to give you an idea of the depth of the desperation of need.

I was talking to her again on the front stoop, and she was talking to me about her heroin use and she was talking to me about the prescription drugs she takes when she can't get the fix she needs. She was describing where she shoots up and why and how she does it to just sort of endure the day. And I said, "What can I do for you? What do you need? Let me do something, I feel so helpless."

She asked me if I would get her some underpants, and she said that her pimp didn't allow her to have any. I knew why, because that's something that is so personal and something that is such an intimate dignity and then to deny somebody that, says at that level of intimacy, you're not worth it and I own you and I control that part of your body. So, to deny her that, well, you can imagine, I was immediately at the store and I'm buying packages. I didn't know what size, I was just grabbing whatever I could, and I drove around for the next three weeks with that in my car...just hoping one day I'd see her again.

Sure enough, one time I was driving into town, and I see her coming out of this chicken restaurant, pulled over to the side of the street, I'm like, "Heather!" She turns around and looks at me, and she remembered me, which I found amazing given the intoxication of our last two encounters.

I said, "I'm so glad to see you. I just want to hug you, and I've got something for you." We walked over to the car, and I pulled out this bag and I just opened the top of the bag to show her what was inside and she started crying and she said, "You remembered." It broke my heart you know, "Of course I remembered it's the only thing you asked of me and it's such a simple thing." She was so grateful.

I didn't see her again for several months, and that's kind of how the relationships go. We tried a couple of times to get her into rehab facilities, but there's something about the street...there's a sense of, "I got this. I can survive out here." There truly is something about having the mastery over the streets to be able to say, "I'm okay, I'm okay, I'm okay, I don't need any help."

DT: What's the connection between drug use and sex trafficking? What is the interplay? You haven't talked much about the sex trafficking or prostitution or the challenge or the coercion or the force or fraud. You talked a lot about the drug use because obviously that's what you experienced with her. What's the interplay?

Jeanne: Yeah. I can only tell you what we see, and part of it is dictated by the context of the trafficking. When we're talking about that area of Baltimore, that is a drug area. The co-mingling of prostitution and drugs arguably is at 95% to 100%, right? Either she's addicted and so she goes down to that area, and she is being forced to work that area to get the drugs to feed her habit that could be the co-mingling. But, in our residential facility at The Samaritan Women, we get individuals who come to us who have been sex trafficked from all over the country, and it could be in Las Vegas casinos, it could be on the Internet, through brothels, through different venues.

On the west coast for example, drug use is not a one-to-one ratio, so I would say in our facility, we probably see that substance abuse is a problem is about 30%. But, here is the interesting thing, even though drugs are incredibly insidious in the way that they held a person captive, we also see remarkable results that when you take a woman out of her constant threat, she no longer needs to escape through substance abuse. And so, we have seen really good examples of people who can say we don't need that anymore because getting through the day isn't as hard as it was.

DT: Makes sense. So, back to Heather. You provided her with these undergarments...what did that do in you? What was your next step after you had this encounter with her?

Jeanne: Well, I'll tell you this whole situation of giving her something that I would consider a basic need did not fill me with a great sense of joy. It actually made me really angry. You can't tell me that it's that desperate and yet, I found out it is.

I had started The Samaritan Women, and I had purchased this property and it's not going to be any comfort to people to know that I didn't have a plan, you know? Because aren't they always telling you - you should have a business plan. I didn't have a plan. I pretty much stumbled into this more based on passion and rage than a thoughtful methodical business case.

First of all, I was scouring across Maryland to find out who's doing something on this issue, and I kept coming up with zero or very, very little. Then, I started looking around nationally, who's doing something about this issue. I began to read that one of the greatest areas of deficit was residential care. And, I think back in that 2007-2008 time frame, there was actually very little even being written about human trafficking in the United States.

I did find a fair amount of literature about Southeast Asia and having grown up in Bangkok, I could connect to that, but that was the bulk of what I was finding. So, it wasn't as if I could say, "Oh, here is a McDonald's and I want to replicate a McDonald's," right? Here is a particular department store and I'm going to make one of those. It was more somebody should do something. I guess I'll do something. What should I do? Well, there should be a place where these ladies go because the frustration of being on the street is overwhelming. I want to take you right now, but I don't know where I'm going to take you. So, I think that's as thoughtful as the business plan was.

The funny story about how I acquired the property is that a girlfriend of mine from church and I had attended a Women of Faith conference and got to talking about how there's no place really for girls who need some deep and long term healing from the trauma in their lives. And so, we collaborated on how we were going to do something together and literally stumbled across this property by accident.

This is not a part of my normal commute pattern. Southwest Baltimore has been known as a very violent crime area and so, we got lost (this was pre-GPS days, so you have to appreciate that). We got lost, and we turned into this driveway of this dilapidated estate and just as we pulled into the road and before we stop to back out, we just sort of have this pause and we both looked at each other with that, "Oh, crap [laughs] where are we? And why – do you feel what I feel?" And we just had this moment of silence in acknowledging that there was something about this place.

She's immediately on the phone, right? Does anybody know about this house? What's going on? We come to find out that the former owner of the property had just passed away and the place was an absolute disrepair. It was a wreck...you could have filmed horror movies here. And, you know, there is something about it that was just so endearing, which probably says a lot about me, right?

We became captivated by this place and what it could be, and that's how we started the ball rolling to find out there was an offer on the property for $1.6 million to turn it into a nursing home. We did not have that in cash, but we took it upon ourselves to go find the heir to whom the property had been bequeathed. He was out in West Virginia, and he's a national horticulturist, fascinating guy, who wasn't the least bit interested in keeping the property. We told him what we wanted to do with it, and we said it was going to be a ministry of healing for women.

We didn't get into sex trafficking per se, but we were just laying out our intent of what we wanted to build and he said, "Is this for the church?" And we said, "Well, it will be faith-based. It will be Christian, but it's not for a particular church, but..." And he pondered for a couple of minutes and he said, "Well, what can you afford?" We kind of conferred and said, "Well, if we leverage everything we have, we could probably come up with about $500,000." And he said, "Okay."

So, he walked away from $1.1 million, and we acquired what might be the last undeveloped parcel of land in the city for a mere pittance. And about four days before settlement, my business partner backed out and that was my "oh crap" moment number two, right? Where you just kind of say, I can't do this alone.

I went to the settlement table prepared to tell them, thank you, but I can't do it. And the owner said, "You know, we're just going to make this a gentleman's agreement. I like what you're doing, I want to help you out and so, pay me when you can." You know that doesn't happen every day.

I'd like to say that I did what every strong woman does in the situation, I signed my life away, and then I sat in the parking lot and cried for a long time realizing what I had just done. That was the beginning and sometimes births are not pretty and so, I really stumbled into this. I just had to make that one step, and then literally hundreds of people in the community and now across the United States have come out in support.

DT: So, you've got the property. Now, what do you do?

Jeanne: Well, the first thing we did was get our non-profit status, so that we can legally operate because by that point I don't have any money. We were going to have to secure some support from the community, and the place was a wreck. Before we could actually start the work, one of the things that we realized was there's such a level of ignorance about sex trafficking in America that we were going to have to grow our volunteer base. You can't just say, hey, come work on this thing that you don't understand and you've never heard of and you think is overseas.

We really went down a parallel track of educating and engaging, concurrent with renovating the property. We were going as far around the state as we could to help people become aware of the issue of sex trafficking in America and then specifically in Maryland which was a real challenge because we didn't have any data. Everybody always wants to know how big is the problem, and we don't know. Here we are five years later, and we still don't have the numbers.

Back to the story...we're using all these community volunteers and that's where it got very exciting because we reached out to volunteer organizations and said hey, there's this new non-profit starting and people would come because they just wanted to see what you were about and then when you could tell them the story, they become captivated. And then, they'd sit there with their jaws open going, "What? Here?"

Connecting with law enforcement locally and nationally has also been really important, because they were our best sources of information. What we did was to learn from them so that we could package it for your average citizen. So, it took us four years and those were really good, fun, tireless years or constantly tired years, because we worked constantly to prepare this place to open in 2012.

Long about fall of 2011, we got a phone call from a law enforcement professional who said, "I have somebody, I think she'd be perfect for your program. Will you take her?" And I'm thinking, "Sure, in about five or six months when we'll be ready." And she said, "No, I mean tomorrow." "What?" She said, "Can you just take her? I've got nothing." That's really important for us to understand. You know we're asking these law enforcement professionals to be out there, and we're all about rescue, but there's nothing on the back end. It's really a false promise to rescue without restoration.

We agreed to take this gal, and she came in and she spoke no English, and this sweet woman showed up with a t-shirt and a little bit of shorts and again, didn't speak any English. Thanks to Google translator, we got what we could, and we were launched.

That's probably not the way I would have started. It would have been nice to have ribbon cuttings ceremony and say that all the beds are dressed, but sometimes you respond when the call is made - not when you're ready. And that had become our groove, respond when you're called. So, that was our first resident.

DT: So now, two years later, tell me about your program and what the residents do on a daily basis?

Jeanne: So, here we are two years later at The Samaritan Women...now at a point where we really understand what we do. It was as if the last couple of years have been a refining process, because we've had the privilege of serving the women who have formed the program.

We are a Christian residential facility that invests in women who have been sex trafficked. We focus on those who have been trafficked domestically, and we take adult females. Now, interestingly, we take women from all over the country. That wasn't our original intent, but as we network particularly with federal law enforcement, we come to find out that there is a dearth of facilities across the country. And so, if somebody five states away finds out there's a residential facility in Maryland, they need a place for their gal. So we've gotten calls from all over...the west coast, the south, and if she's the right fit for our program, we take her.

So, what's the right fit? Well, our bed capacity is fourteen, so comparatively that's a relatively large program. We allow the ladies to stay up to two years, because our goal is to be a restorative program. We're not a rescue program. We work with rescue programs, but when the woman is in a place where her threat has been so mitigated or reduced that she can begin to focus on herself. You can't say, "what do you want to do with your life" when you're running. You can't say, "what are your hobbies...what are your goals" when you're in trauma and terror. So, we have to take a woman who has had those issues dissipated.

When a woman comes into our program, she has a ninety-day assessment window where she exhales to detox and decompress. By detox, I don't necessarily mean substance. Sometimes you have to detox from your thought patterns, your relationships, your behaviors, you have to let a lot go in order to have a new life. So the first ninety days is really that time where we say it's safe, and you can let it go and you can put some of those things down now.

We see magical things happen in those ninety days...just amazing things when you let the human spirit stop being afraid and you give it opportunity to grow. The kinds of ideas and dreams and aspirations that come out of these ladies has helped to change our program because we don't start from day one going, well, you should want to be a home health aide or sobriety counselor or work at McDonald's or – no, let's wait, let's give her that breathing room of self-discovery and then delight in the kinds of things that she comes up with on her own.

We've found that investing in a lot of our ladies with a culinary arts program seems to be a very comfortable profession for them. They love the idea that they can create and serve. It's a gift they haven't had in their life. To be able to go to our farm and pick tomatoes and then make a spaghetti sauce and then serve others is a whole life experience that you don't have when you're out there on the streets.

We invest in them also in terms of entrepreneuring, and so that's where the excitement comes where women discover their gifts. Because of the limitations that they have with legal issues, financial issues, education issues, the world of micro-enterprise is actually very available to them. In America, we send money overseas and say, well, why don't we help this person run a small business so that they can teach them how to fish, right? But we don't do enough of that in our own country.

That's part of what our ladies have taught us and helped to inform our program. We're doing a lot more with entrepreneuring now, which is really exciting seeing these women launch businesses.

DT: Take me through your holistic approach that includes medical, spiritual, and psychological. What are all of the things that you're offering beyond just a safe home?

Jeanne: Very early on, we realized that you can't just attend to one aspect of a person, because all of these elements of her past, her future, and her present are all intertwined with her physical being, her spiritual being, her emotional stability. So our program is based on five pillars. First, we invest in self-care, because so many of the women that we see come in having been traumatized from a very young age...four, five, eight years old. Life is literally chaos from elementary school to the present.

They have missed a lot of the things that you and I take for granted. So we make sure she knows how to take care of herself. We make sure we are coaching her on how she can take care of a domestic environment, how she can take care of her own health and hygiene. We make sure that she's enrolled in services, and she has the medical treatment or dental treatment. Certainly, the therapeutic care is woven throughout what we do, so she'll meet with counselors and go to group and those types of things. So self-care is first and foremost.

Then, we begin to look at the relational aspects of her life, because she has to let go of some relationships, and we want to build a foundation for her forming new relationships, relationships based on different values. The relational brokenness that they come with has to be attended to. Spirituality is a part of everything we do. It is a part of the way we talk, and it's a part of the way we walk because we are all spiritual beings.

In our program, a woman doesn't have to be our religion to be a part of the program. We've had ladies who are agnostic and atheist and Muslim and Jewish, and that's all fine. We just want to be respected for who we are, and we will respect them for who they are. But, this is who we are.

And so, we walk it out, because there's something to be gained for all of us in just demonstrating integrity with your life.

Academics are a part of her readiness. When she's ready, if it's a matter of getting her high school education, then we're going to bring in tutors who will invest in her for her GED. If she's ready to go further than that and she wants to look at community college or a license or certificate programs, we're going to find the resources and amass the resources for her to do that.

The vocational piece is the piece that's important, but later, because frankly, until you've arrested some of these other issues in her life, you can't be fixed on what are you going to do to make money. Because you know what? If you start there, you're merely speaking the language of where she came from: "You better hurry up and makes the money" - because it's all about what you can make.

We want to delay that question for as long as possible, and that's why women stay at our program at no cost and they don't have to have money to be here because, we want to work from the inside to the outside.

DT: Take me through an average day for the women. What is day to day like look like for them?

Jeanne: Well, we're all at the dining room table at 8 o'clock in the morning, and that is our time for devotions to just get the day off on a positive start. And we do some Bible study, we do some sharing, praises with each other really to just uplift.

Breakfast. Then, they go out into chores, everybody has responsibilities in the home because we're teaching as well as helping them feel a part of this place. There's counseling scheduled for them individually throughout the day, and then in the afternoon, they go into working on their individual concerns. So if her goal is a GED, she's meeting with a tutor. If this gal's goal is she's working on a job opportunity or a vocation, she'll do that.

In the evenings, we all come back together for programming, and it's a different program each night. It can be anything from movie night to Bible study to our support group to goal setting, financial literacy classes, but that's the time that we're together. And then, the weekends, you know, we do a normal people do on a weekends. We go places, we do things, we take care of the house, and we go on outings. Sometimes we get tickets to concerts, and we do what normal people do.

DT: This is your life... it sounds like this is your total...

Jeanne: All consuming passion, and I can say that with delight now. [laughs] But, there have been days that have been really, really long. I think what I've realized personally is if you don't throw your whole heart into something, I'll be back to where I was when I started...chasing something after something on the outside instead of being driven by what's on the inside. So, yeah, it's every waking moment and every sleeping moment of my life, but I wouldn't...I wouldn't change it.

DT: Talk to me about the property and the farm. How does the farm operate? Who takes care of it? Where do the fruits of the labor go?

Jeanne: We're very blessed to have this enormous property, and there was nothing happening when we acquired the place. With all of this land which is under an environmental easement, we can't build on it, so what are you going to do? Well, let's make the land work for us. Somebody suggested gardening, and I'm originally from Illinois and I wasn't really into farming. What's been amazing is we did proceed with the idea of establishing an urban farm, and that has brought community members out in droves. We get school buses of children, we get college groups, fraternities and sororities and churches, civic groups coming out to grow in this urban environment. Then, we've gotten to a point where we just donate the produce into the inner city to combat the issue of urban food deserts.

We continue to have the idea that it would be a place where the ladies would engage with the farm, but there is something incredibly intimidating about the farm and so we have to move carefully on that. You know if somebody's led a very urban life and you take them into this open space, it can be daunting. We start small with things in the greenhouse and potted plants and florals and things like that and engage the ladies. They love going out and getting the eggs from the chickens, and that's a good deal of fun.

The farm is largely our gift back to the community. So, it's the community that comes in and does the growing, and then we turn it around and make it a gift back to the community.

DT: Tell me how this is changing individual lives. Whose life has been turned around?

Jeanne: One of the things that we're struggling with in this whole work against sex trafficking in America is what does it mean to have a success. By and large, we don't really know. Outside of this particular issue, we have our preconceived ideas of what success is supposed to look like. And, with no diminishment of hope, I want you to understand that when I say that success looks like functional brokenness. That's going to sound really peculiar, because most of us cannot conceive of the layers and layers of trauma and relational brokenness and spiritual wounding and mental illness and substance abuse that these women have endured.

We're now looking at success incrementally and not as a composite. Success doesn't mean she's got a job and she's married and she has children and she's driving an SUV. That's not success. Success means that she has begun to connect to community again. You have to understand in sex trafficking, you are taking a human being and you are dehumanizing them and manufacturing a human into a product.

You actually have to disconnect them from their humanity in order to productize. We have to reverse that process. We have to now take somebody who believes she's a product and show her her humanity. Her humanity and our humanity.

What that looks like is success. That looks like our ladies every Friday going to the soup kitchen, and they're serving others. They don't have a dime, but they can give. That looks like when our girls go to the children's home or to the school next to us, and they hold the Christmas party for the kids whose parents are incarcerated. Even if they've been incarcerated, now they can give back.

That could mean when we have a gal like Rose who celebrated her 22nd birthday with us and admitted to us on that day that she'd never had a birthday party. We keep a placard on our wall...it's actually just a sheet of paper that we write on that says the "firsts" that you've done at The Samaritan Women. They will write things like "it's the first time I've ever seen a chicken...or it's the first time I've ever cooked a meal." We've had women where this was the first time they've ever sat at a table and eaten a meal with others because all their life they've eaten out of bag or box.

Success at The Samaritan Women looks like when a woman discovers that she has something to give. When our ladies sit around, and they are taught how to knit and they know one particular knitting technique and so, they make scarves. Well, that's exciting, but here is the humanity piece, they don't keep it, they give the product away, they give it to somebody else because they have generativity and generosity. And so, success looks like the movement back into being a member of society, and for each gal that's going to look a little bit different, but it's all worth celebrating.

DT: Tell me what you can about one of the ladies we met today...Rocky.

Jeanne: She is twenty and she came to us as an out-of-state referral from an agency that had heard about what we were doing, and their law enforcement connection said she had just put her trafficker away and needed to start over. That chapter of her life was now coming to a close, and she had no idea how to start afresh.

She came to us as a real leap of faith on her part and had only been with us for a couple of months when we begin to discover that one of her passions is to go to culinary school. We thought, well, that's great because we have culinary arts program. And just in exploring what are the things that you like to do, she says, "I just love making things for other people. I would just love to serve." And, in preparation for the holidays, we said, "What are you going to make for everybody else?" She said, "I'm going to make a cheesecake." We were all happy with that answer. We said, "Oh, you know, they're kind of hard. Do you make a good cheesecake?" "I make a mean cheesecake." So we said, "You're on, babe. Make us a mean cheesecake. Let's see what you got." It was awesome. It was spectacular.

That just started this brainstorming of...I bet other people would be interested in this cheesecake, I bet our board members would want you to make a cheesecake for them, I bet other people, you know, there are people out there who would pay a lot of money and then all of a sudden ding, ding, ding, ding, ding, right? The idea started going.

We said we have an event coming up, why don't you make some cheesecakes of different varieties and we'll just lay out the samples and let people sample them. And, she did it, and in two days she sold thirty-five cheesecakes. She is flying high right now. She has launched her business, and now we have a woman in the community who is a marketing expert who's going to come in and mentor with her to help her put the packaging of her business together. And so, hopefully you will begin to see her website on all of her retailing coming to fruition.

Those are the kinds of stories that we want to see replicated here. Discover what is innate and unique and special about her, and then give her the environment where it can flourish, because happiness and contentment and purpose will come if you create the right environment.

DT: When you think about Maryland and Baltimore County, what are your hopes and dreams for the next ten years? What do you want to see in your county...in your state?

Jeanne: As I think of my hopes for Maryland, I could be really practical and say, we need X number of facilities in these demographic areas, and we need everybody to be on board legislatively, and we need an informed citizenry...and absolutely we need those things to happen.

Let me bring it up to perhaps a loftier level. Baltimore, in the greater metro area, is fascinating, because it is an area that has rich history and a lot of resources that have been neglected, mismanaged, abused, discarded. Baltimore is one particular city in America poised perfectly for a renaissance. Right now, the public reputation of Baltimore is "The Wire", and it's not a positive reputation.

The reason I think it's so interesting that we are planted here in this particular city is because you can take the story of Baltimore and you can take the story of what we're doing at The Samaritan Women and the property and what we've done to reconstruct this, and then you can take the story of these women's lives, and you see three potential parallels of a city, an organization or property, and a person who reached a desperate low. With the right investment of love and energy, all of them can reach restoration. So I think it's no accident that we're in Baltimore.

DT: What can the average person do in their city across America about this issue? You've got teachers, you've got moms, you've got some legislators, some law enforcement, you've got average people, you've got business people like yourself...what can they do?

Jeanne: Everybody involved in this work is going to tell you that the first step is always learning...get educated. But, that's kind of frustrating because I could say, "Okay, America go get educated," and you walk away going, "I have no idea what that means." Right? "I don't know how to do that." Let me be real practical. Go online and look up either human trafficking or sex trafficking in your area. Go on the federal websites connect with the agencies, there are coalitions across the United States that are working on this issue. There are task forces. You can contact your local FBI or Homeland Security or local law enforcement and say who's doing what on this issue, and then ask those agencies what they need.

I'm not going to be prescriptive and say whatever agency needs. I can tell you what we need. We need all of you to knock on our door, e-mail us, call us, and say, "What do you need?"

The appeal that I will make nationally is for housing. You might have a house that you'd be willing to donate to a non-profit organization, and here's a group of people who just don't have the real estate, but they have the will. Put those two together. You can donate financially to anybody who is trying to start a home.

In our region, there are cases that involve a potential of fifty or more victims who are going to need some kind of care. Our agency alone is only fourteen beds. Where are those other thirty-six ladies or children or men going to go? You can be a part of the housing issue. Come alongside those agencies that are already starting shelter programs, or jump in with me and be a part of starting one in your community.

DT: That's great. Anything else? Anything else that's really on your heart that you wanted to share?

Jeanne: My learning has evolved, and so I want everybody to be patient with the fact that you are going to learn about this issue on one level and then as you pursue it, you're going to find that it is the proverbial onion being peeled. You will learn layers and layers, and it will become daunting because you'll realize, oh, my gosh there's all this problem with the law and legislation, oh, my goodness, what are we going to do about pornography. This is related to domestic violence, this is related to child abuse, this is related to substance abuse. Where do we connect in public health? Where do we connect in mental health?

It's going to be so tempting to just cup your ears and say, "I can't engage, it's too much."

I'm asking you to pick any one of those. We have a lot of disparate pieces that are not connected and it is worthy for you to engage in any one of them. So, if your heart is to work on the "demand" side, so that you put us out of business, go with my blessing. There are so many ways that people can engage...pick something...it's all needed.

The Samaritan Women
Baltimore, MD
www.thesamaritanwomen.org

The Samaritan Women is a national Christian organization providing restorative care to survivors, and bringing about an end to domestic human trafficking through awareness, prevention, and advocacy.

HEATHER

Sex Trafficking Survivor

While growing up in rural Maryland, Heather began experimenting with drugs, alcohol, and her own sexuality as she sought the attention that was missing at home. Experimentation eventually led to an addiction to heroin and a friendship with a young man who turned her own to the city of Baltimore.

By manipulating her with pseudo-love and promises of a better life, her "boyfriend" convinced her to start stripping on The Block - an area of the city with a dozen or more strip clubs all in a row. On the first night, stripping quickly turned into prostitution, and all the money would land in her boyfriend's pockets.

Years later, a casual encounter with Jeanne Allert would begin to put Heather's life on a different path.

DT: Tell me what life was like growing up...

Heather: I grew up in rural Maryland, which at the time the only things were a Kmart, a McDonald's, Harvest Inn Family Restaurant, and a gas station...so pretty much country.

My parents divorced young, but my mom became a banker. We lived in a four-bedroom house, and we didn't want for anything. I grew up well, and I have a sister and a brother. My brother is quite a bit older, but me and my sister were very, very close growing up, because on the weekends, we went to my dad's house...so literally every day we were together. We're two years apart. We look a lot alike.

Now that I'm an adult, I realize my mom worked two jobs to pay the bills, and I appreciate her that for that today.

DT: What was school like for you?

Heather: I did dance. I took ballet, tap, and jazz for nine years. I was in cheerleading in ninth grade. I was voted 'best dressed' in my eleventh grade year. I was what you would probably call preppy in high school. There's really not much to do in high school there.

But, you know, there's bonfires and just a lot of kids getting into drinking and drugs. And, around the age of fourteen is when I started drinking, and my mom worked a lot, so I had parties at my house a lot. I realized I craved attention, and I could be the one who out-drank everybody including guys older than me. I had low self-esteem, and got into the drug scene.

DT: When you say "got in the drug scene", how did that impact you?

Heather: Well, when I was still in high school, my mom and dad realized there was a serious problem. When a friend and I got caught smoking in the bathroom, and they found heroin on her...but I didn't get caught.

So, my next class, they called me out, and the principal came and took me to the office, and the state police were there. They looked through all my stuff and found the syrup. They took it very seriously...told my mom there's letters about doing heroin, and I think that's when my parents realized there was something seriously wrong.

I really didn't take it as being serious, because I wasn't a heroin addict, you know. I wasn't using needles, but I was experimenting with a lot of drugs. I was promiscuous, I would say. I had sex with guys who would give me attention.

Pretty much when I was about sixteen or seventeen, I started doing heroin more, and I just remember my mom really tell me I had to leave. I remember her crying, and I would go around like a crazy person slamming doors, begging for money. And so, at the age of seventeen, I met a guy who is now actually about to go to court for a murder charge, and he turned me on to the city. That's pretty much where my life went downhill from there.

DT: When you say he turned you on to the city, what does that mean?

Heather: Well, when I was eighteen, I went there. There's a place in Baltimore called "The Block", and it is a series of about ten or twelve strip clubs. It used to be a lot bigger, but it's more consolidated now. I was talked into going there, and I thought it was just to be a stripper. Little did I know there would be the day when I would do my first trick, date, whatever you want to call it. And...

DT: Let me back up on that, because that's a pretty big transition from – you're seventeen and you're having some challenges with your mom to doing your first trick. Who invited you to go to "The Block"? Was it that friend? Was it somebody else? And, why were you open to becoming a stripper?

Heather: Well, at the time, you know, the boyfriend that I told you about that was older, he would go and steal things and take care of me. We ended up getting caught, and he got like a three, four-year sentence. So, I basically was on my own now and didn't know what to do.

DT: What did you Mom think about all of this?

Heather: She finally did the tough love thing, and she was trying to get me locked up. Eventually, I did get locked up, because he had stolen a car, and I was in it, so that was a way for my mom to get me put away for ninety days.

When I came out, he was still in jail. I was eighteen by this point, and I went and met a new boyfriend. I was struggling, and I wanted to steal. It just wasn't something that I was good at.

I was open to stripping, and he connived me into it even though later to find out it was prostitution. He said, "All you have to do is get up there. You don't have to even get completely naked, and you make hundreds of dollars a day. My ex-girlfriend did it."

I had actually been in a recovery house for a short period, and I heard girls talking about working there and prostituting, and that's where The Block came into effect.

DT: When you went to The Block, did you apply for a job?

Heather: Seriously, when you walk in...as long as you look somewhat okay, you're hired on the spot. There's underage girls working there. You have an outfit on, and go out there and make quick money. I learned that day that really it's not about dancing at all. You may make $20 in tips on the stage, but there's an upstairs or downstairs depending on the club. The bartender basically told me about "bottles"...that's what they call them. You can do what you want with the guys. Go upstairs, and we'll give you a condom. And, I wasn't prepared for this.

DT: When you say the bartender said they have "bottles"...help me understand what that means.

Heather: It's a word they use if a cop comes in. A guy buys a "bottle" so he can drink with you, but the drink consists of five minutes of conversation. That drink is to convince a guy to either get a lap dance or go upstairs, and you would have thirty minutes to an hour for about $250.

That's what a bottle basically means. You don't get champagne, I mean if you ask they might give it to you, but I've never gotten champagne. It's just their word for it.

DT: So, the first night you're there, and somebody buys you a bottle, did you realize what was happening?

Heather: I thought I was going to be able to just go upstairs, and that I would somehow just try to not have sex, but the guy wanted to have sex. At the point, I have a heroin addiction and I ended up – ended up having sex with him.

DT: And then, from that point, how did that transition? Did you continue to work there, or did your boyfriend at time transition you into another situation?

Heather: No, he didn't help me into a better situation...he lived off me. I supported him, and I kept working there until a point when I got tired of supporting him. While I was prostituting myself and I decided I was going to go home to my mom, and my mom didn't know I was a stripper. She didn't know that I was shooting heroin or snorting heroin.

She let me come home, and he thought I was probably going to be there when I got off work but I wasn't. For once, I went through with something I was going to do, and my mom came and picked me up.

I got kicked out for doing drugs, and I ended up going to the rehab. When I got out, I went in a recovery house, and I started doing dates on Wilkins Avenue and…

DT: Is that something you chose to do or someone?

Heather: Another girl at the recovery house told me that it's fast money. It was hard, because when you're there…you're not getting any money and, you know, it sounds stupid, it was like kind of revolving door like, okay, if I – if I'm prostituting I might as well get high, why not do it together, you know?

I just can remember getting with guys that were so grotesque, and it was pretty much like the bottom of the barrel. I met this guy who was trying to be a pimp, and he took me to a truck stop and said, "I'm going to make you a lot more money than you're making in the street." And, he is actually the father of my daughter.

He was older. He was about forty-five years old, and at one point in his prime, he had five kids. I was his only girl at the time. Well, at the time, you know, he had other pimp friends, and I met this guy who told me that he knows this better truck stop. I'm going to take you to Atlantic City, and by this point, I have my daughter. He got me so brainwashed, you know, he gave me so much attention at first like you're beautiful and taking me shopping and doing my nails and, you know, made me feel special.

The new guy took me to the truck stop, but he ended up getting money from me because he had a girl…a bottom bitch. When you have a pimp, bottom bitch is the girl that makes most money and gets the most attention.

He'll sleep with you and not the other girls, and meanwhile I'm giving him pedicures and doing his nails and fixing him dinner and staying out. Meanwhile, I'm just so brainwashed thinking he's so in love with me and, you know, like really thinking he cares about me. And, I have my daughter there with me, so you know what I mean? I felt like I could have my cake and eat it, too. In Atlantic City, I remember making $1,200 and handing every penny over to him. He had me so brainwashed.

Until I met some Christian friends, I would say that it wasn't his fault that I got pimped. It was me, because I wanted to be able to keep my daughter and do what I was doing.

Now I know that he brainwashed me. Who in their right mind would just hand that kind of money?

He was an old school pimp, and he had one girl for like almost twenty years. I remember him telling her "we're going to get your son", but they never got her son. I wish someone could have told me that there's so much more to life than what you're doing. [cries]

Even now as far as I know, he's old and dying, and he's just now letting her get her GED so she'll have something when he's gone. I mean, what do you have? He took you from your family, and I remember him just beating her – beating her all the time. He didn't beat me yet, and I was like – and she would say things and she knew it would get him mad. It's like she wanted to get beaten. I don't know.

DT: What was your relationship like with him? How did that relationship play out over the course of three years?

Heather: He got my trust. Like I said, the other girl would get beat, and he hadn't beat me yet. And, I was bottom bitch and...

DT: You talked about him brainwashing you...how did that happen?

Heather: I think it's over a series, you know, not right away. Right away, I realized that I am giving this man everything, but it's for my daughter. As time went on, he bought me more and more things, bought me a car, put me in my own apartment.

It made me feel like I was loved and got attention...something I didn't get from my mom when I was little, because she was working all the time.

Took me a long time to realize that I crave that attention just as I craved it as a child. And, it get to a point when my wife-in-law, that's what they call the other women. If you have a pimp, any other girls are your wife-in-laws.

So, my wife-in-law was in jail, so we decided to go to Orlando during Christmas time. We decided to go to Orlando and make money. There's a lot of money in Orlando, and when I was there, you're going to stay out 'til you make a certain amount of money, and you're not coming back until then.

We had money, but in Orlando, it was harder to find heroin than in Baltimore. I was very dope sick, and I didn't want to go out and have to trick sick. I got to a rock bottom point being ill and having to do something sexual with men. I got mad, and I slammed the door shut and I said, "I can't believe you're making me do this when I'm sick like this." I slammed the door shut, and he said, "Get back in the car right now."

He started driving in silence, and then he started screaming and said, "I'm taking you to Baltimore." He used to threaten me by saying, "You make me so mad that I'm afraid I'm going to kill you one day. You are out of pocket." That's what he called it when you're not doing too great. You're out of pocket, you're talking out of pocket. And I remember him threatening, "I'm going to put a hot curling iron up your…" I don't have to say where it is, but up inside of you.

I truly believed he would and could have done that. He didn't, but I truly believe it was an event that could and would happen. I just remember him saying, "I've got to take you to Baltimore, because I'm going to end up killing you." And on the way, the guy we were trying to buy heroin from called back, and my pimp said, "Do you want it? Do you want it? You want me to turn around?" And I said, "Yeah," at the time, and that was the first time I got hit.

He used to know how to hit just right, so it wouldn't mess up your face. He hit me so hard in the side of my head, I saw stars and I passed out after so many blows to the head. I had a knot on my head like this, but it kept me pretty as he said. And he said, "You're making me do this to you. You're making me do this to you." And, at the time I believed it. I was so brainwashed by that point that I believed it. And so, once he started hitting me, it kept going.

After seeing my wife-in-law get beat time and time again, I tried not to do things like that. I always made more money than her, because at the time she was forty years old, she had been with him for twenty years. I made a lot more money than her usually. But, he – I know he had done very evil things in the past, I mean he told me that.

A girl he picked up in Georgia or South Carolina and taken to Baltimore ran to the police officer and said she had been kidnapped, and he was trying to make her go out and prostitute. I think he said he had two kidnapping charges and pimping and pandering charges on his record. He says it wasn't true, but I believe it was because I know what he's capable of.

He had me so brainwashed at one point, I got caught with my pictures up on Craigslist, and it was a human trafficking group that thought I was underage. I went to go do a date from on Craigslist and the guy thought I was underage, but I was like 22 at the time.

And they said, well, we know you have a pimp. They said, "He's got a kidnapping charge and pimping and pandering. Come on, give him up." And, you know, it wasn't the police from Maryland. They were some kind of task force who goes to other states.

It was a real embarrassment to me when my mom called me up and said, "You're in the paper for prostitution and got paid $250 at a hotel, and we find out from your sister who heard about it on a radio."

They let me go, and they told me that I had seven days to turn in underage girls with my pimp. He had me so brainwashed at that point, I took the charge and ended up doing six months, for what? You know when you leave a pimp, all you leave is with clothes on your back. You know all these clothes you buy every day, they're for you to look good on the street. He doesn't really care about you. I staying with him on and off for three years, because I chose other pimps. They used to call me "Choosy Susie", because I would choose other pimps. It's like a name they made up.

Anyway, I would pick other pimps that I thought were better. One beat on me, and another tried to recruit me by saying "I'll let you put the car in your name" and this and that. It never happened, but they used different ways to get to you and that happened in D.C.

DT: Did you ever fear for your life when you were working?

Heather: Yeah, in 2006, I was in Atlantic City, and there was a killer picking up girls with blonde hair. They found them in this ditch by these cheap hotels that are off the main strip of Atlantic City, and it was like national news. I think that was God, because I have blonde hair you know. It only would have been probably a matter of time that he would have driven by me and picked me up. You know what I mean? I've had a lot of moments and when my faith has grown over the years.

My parents never put religion on me. My dad was Catholic and he was against it because of what he saw as a kid. But, my faith has grown, and I believe everything happens for a reason...even bad things. I should be dead and I'm not and I sit here today.

I've had cops pick me up and show me a badge on a work shirt, and they make me do stuff. They'd say, "As long as you do it, we're not going to arrest you." I've been raped.

I lived everywhere from a tent in Baltimore City to a mansion for a short period of my life. I got with this very older gentleman who they used to call "Rolls Royce Bob", and he had a mansion. I had a tanning room when I stayed there. So, I've been from the bottom of the bottom to the top of the top.

And, same thing with prostitution. I've been to Wilkins Avenue to Atlantic City, Las Vegas, and Orlando. I've been through a lot in my 28 years.

DT: Tell me about your encounter with Jeanne Allert. What were you doing and what happened when this lady walked up to you?

Heather: Jeanne is awesome. I was prostituting on a Sunday. I'm walking to the avenue, and she was in this van. She used to go along with a couple of other individuals that have all gone different ways now. They all had a common purpose of trying to help women that were on the streets. The day I met her she said, "You come up in this house and take a shower" and that time I was at the bottom of the bottom as far as prostitution. You know there are such pretty girls from all walks of life out there.

I remember her asking me how she could help, and I said I needed underwear. I actually remember her telling me that she wasn't going to buy me a certain kind of underwear, and every time she would see me when I was on Wilkins Avenue, I would always ask for more underwear.

She ended up being an awesome woman who has really inspired me to be the person I am today, and I love her like another mother. I call her my other mommy. She inspired me and showed me that there are real people in this world, Christian people. She took me in her house when I was a drug addict and trusted me in her home. She just does awesome work, and I'm really happy that she has this house that she helps women in human trafficking now because it's perfect.

She's helped me so much. She's the one that told me that my pimp had brainwashed me, and I thought about it and that was the truth, really.

DT: How did you transition out? How did you leave your pimp for the last time and how did you begin to create a new life?

Heather: I met Jeanne and other Christian people, and I actually had gone to jail. I believe I was born again, and I saw there's more to my life, you know. I took a class in there, and it was about what you're supposed to be like for God...not like as a job...like what's your purpose...what's God's purpose for you.

Ever since then, I'm just inspired, started going to church, I got myself to recovery and I just, you know, I'm always telling people about the Lord. And it's really thanks to Jeanne and through other people I'd say that have totally given to me. I always thought of the Bible as too confusing, but my life is just so different today you know.

When I met Jeanne, I wore children size clothes literally, I weighed about 97 pounds, and I looked like hell. Today, I weigh about 100 pounds more, but I have an awesome boyfriend and awesome support system, awesome family, and awesome Christian friends.

DT: Tell me about your boyfriend. How did you meet him?

Heather: My boyfriend, Bobby, we actually lived on the same street growing up, but he was five years older than me. I actually went on Facebook, and I found his picture and he friend requested me. We knew each other we had talked to each other, but we weren't friends or boyfriend/girlfriend.

And I said, wow, because he has pictures of babies, and I said, wow, who-ever got you because he was always a sweetheart. I said, wow, whoever got you is lucky – lucky woman and your kids are beautiful. He wrote back that day instantly, "Oh, they are not my kids. I don't have any kids. I don't have a girlfriend, but I have my own house and my own car." God, I love him.

So, we went on a date. You know how long had it been since I went on a date? Like a real date, not a date as in prostitution – a date. He took me to Little Italy and took me on the paddleboats, and we had our first kiss.

He is very inspirational for me, because he knows about my past. I wanted him to know my past. He knows my story. He doesn't really like talking about it. Bobby has been awesome especially on days when I just want to give in. My pimp tried to contact me again, and Bobby is like, "You're not doing that." I love him from my heart.

DT: How does Bobby and your relationship with him represent a new season for you?

Heather: He inspires me to be a better person, honestly. People used to make fun of him for like dumb stuff. When someone does something I'm quick to fire fight, you know, and he is such a – I don't know, I feel very blessed that God put him in my life, because girls really lost chances with not giving him a chance.

He's, you know, kind of reserved, but I told him right away, you don't ever have to be embarrassed with me. You can say whatever you want with me, and I'll never judge you.

DT: What do you hope for in your future? You got a great future in front of you, what do you dream of? What do you hope for?

Heather: I always wanted to be a nurse. I always wanted to help people. And I want to inspire people and let them know that instead of drugs and human trafficking, there is life.

My hopes are...if not to be a nurse, a counselor...and me and Bobby want a family. I have a daughter, not with him, but he accepts her, and we want to have kids, get married.

As a kid, I used to say I wanted ten kids. I don't want ten kids, but, you know, I want as many as the Lord gives me. And after getting married and I just aspire to be a good mother. Hopefully just if I could help one person, you know, that will make my life worth living.

DT: Do you think a home like The Samaritan Women could have helped you?

Heather: Unfortunately, when I met Jeanne, she told me the idea for the house. I just can't believe how immaculate it is now, but it was just ruins. I just wish it was open when I needed it. When that's over, you still are scarred. You know what I mean? You need time and people like Jeanne to help you.

I think it would have immensely helped me to have counseling. You know, it shouldn't have happened, and I think that houses like these are just amazing, and I am so proud of Jeanne.

DT: If you had the chance to talk to the average person in America, families, professionals, hardworking people who are just becoming aware of this issue, how would you call them to action? What would you want them to do? What would you want them to know?

Heather: You may just drive by going to the gas station, and you see these girls in heels getting in the trucks. Why don't you call the police? A lot of these girls are forced into it and are scared to leave their pimps.

I mean like right in front of you it's happening everywhere. In D.C. just a few miles from the White House, there's pimps and there's girls in barely anything and people see that, and they just turn their back. And I think people need to open their mouths, call the police. The police need to say, "Are you with the pimp? Do you need to get out of situation?" like "It's okay, you're not going to get hurt."

I know people see it, and they just – they don't want to get involved. Just take a risk, because it's helping somebody, saving somebody's life. That's all I would wish.

BUTTON

Sex Trafficking Survivor

While many victims of sex trafficking come from a challenged socio-economic background, there are some who come from middle and upper class families. Although Button grew up in a comfortable home environment with an educated, intact, healthy family, she became defiant in her teenage years, grades slipped, lying became the norm, and she developed a new circle of friends. As her behavior began to spin out of control, her parents sent her to five different counselors, two psychiatrists, and a neurological doctor. Something was missing from her life, and this created a vulnerability for others to prey upon.

After surviving a treacherous experience on the west coast for years, she finally began to get the help she needed at The Samaritan Women in Baltimore, Maryland. It turns out that she isn't bipolar and doesn't need to be medicated or institutionalized. She's receiving counseling to deal with her fears, engage her emotions, and dig deep to figure out why she thought she was never worthy of happiness. She is taking college classes and is very involved with her church.

DT: You mentioned that you grew up in a rather comfortable home environment. When did things begin to change for you?

Button: When I was 15 turning 16, my grandpa died of lung cancer. He was really close to me. And, at the same time he died, my boyfriend was verbally and emotionally abusive, and then he broke up with me. So, I just felt between my grandpa dying and then my boyfriend switching up on me and breaking up with me, I was just alone.

DT: In the midst of kind of feeling alone and obviously the grief of both of those losses, what did you do? What were some of the next steps that led to challenging experiences in your life?

Button: I just started lying to my parents more, not coming home at curfew, disappearing for weekends, started dating different types of people that weren't the best for me, put me in dangerous situations and it actually led my parents to send me to a rehab several states away.

DT: So you were experimenting with drugs?

Button: No drugs. I drank a little bit, but it was mostly that I was emotionally unstable, and the rehab I went to was a dual diagnostic center where they did chemical dependency care and also psychiatric care.

DT: So, did you stick that out or what happened at the end of your stay there?

Button: I did. I was eighteen at the time, so I wasn't focused particularly on fixing myself. It was coed and so there were guys there. But, I did graduate the program, and my parents helped me move to California for another transitional program, and I stayed there for about eight months. Then, I got an apartment, but once I got an apartment after the transitional program, that's when I still was dating people who weren't the best for me.

DT: As you're dating these individuals, was there a particular person you began to connect with that really took you down the road that maybe wasn't one you anticipated?

Button: Yes, it is. I was dating him for a while, and he was acting like my boyfriend. My landlord and her daughter went out of town for a weekend, and I invited him over. Later down the road, I found out he's the one who stole from my landlord, but at the time I was dating him, I didn't know that because I left him there when I went to run some errands. When I got back, he acted like someone broken in the house.

Of course when my landlord came back in town, she kicked me out, and my parents were the ones paying rent and had the rental agreement with her. My parents stopped talking to me, because they were mad at me and I have nowhere else to go, but to move in with that guy.

DT: As you moved in with him, what was that experience like?

Button: At first, it was nice, he still acted as my boyfriend, took me out to dinner and bought me gifts. And then, one day he just came home with what he called a friend's clothes that he borrowed, because he said we were short on money. It turned out to be stripper heels and stripper clothes.

DT: And so, when he brought those to you, did he ask you to wear them?

Button: He told me to try them on and since we were short on money, he knew of a place I could go to make like money and help our situation.

DT: What were you feeling or thinking at the time?

Button: I was confused and I kind of felt sad and lonely, because I felt I put my trust in him. I'm already not talking to my parents and lost the responsibility of having my own place to live, but I felt I had no other choice.

DT: Did you go ahead and follow through with that, or what happened next?

Button: I did. I followed through with dancing in California with him for a while, and then his dad came to town to visit him. And his dad ended up getting sick, and he wasn't home, so he called me when I was at the strip club and told me to go see his dad in the hospital. And when I got there, there was another girl already in the room, and she had the same exact jewelry on that I had on, so he bought both of us the same jewelry. I found out she was actually his girlfriend.

DT: So you're in the hospital room with his dad who's not doing well, and this other woman is there. Was there a confrontation or...?

Button: No, she was very nice. She just asked me questions, and I'm not a confrontational person. I more or less kind of broke down and cried a little bit and knew that I wanted to leave him, but knew I had nowhere else to go and my parents still weren't talking to me.

DT: Did you go ahead and leave?

Button: Once I met another guy, I did.

DT: And that guy, was he a boyfriend?

Button: He said he was a boyfriend, but he also had me working in the strip clubs.

DT: How many years did that go on for?

Button: That was probably a year and a half, because the guy I was with, the strip club money wasn't enough so he actually put me on the tracks in California.

DT: For someone who doesn't know what the "track" is, can you describe what happens?

Button: He drops me off on a street where cars would drive by as I'm walking and pick me up for services in exchange for money.

DT: And, the whole time, he's having you do this...the way you're talking about it feels kind of...a little bit disconnected from the horrendous experience...

Button: Yeah.

DT: So, is he physically forcing you to do this? Is he telling you, you should do this if you love me? Help me understand what's going on inside of your head.

Button: Yeah, he was a pretty good manipulator. I fall in love or lust easily, and he knew I cared about him a lot. He would tell me, "Your family doesn't talk to you, you don't have anywhere else to go, you don't know anybody, you are already working in strip clubs, so you might as well just continue to do it, you could get out soon, it's an easier way to pay for college and then your parents will talk to you again." So, he was very manipulative and brainwashing.

DT: The first time you go into the strip club and you're hired, what was that experience like for you?

Button: Nerve-wracking. I didn't know how to dance at all, so the DJ was very nice to me and told me when I felt comfortable, I could go up on stage and dance. But, the girls weren't nice. They're very catty, and they judge you on your hair, your nails, your makeup, so I felt very uncomfortable. My shift was eight hours, and it took about five hours before I got on stage and I didn't do any private dances that night at all.

DT: After that year and a half of dancing, your boyfriend started dropping you off on the street to make money?

Button: He told me if I really cared about him and I wanted to stay with him that I would do it for him, but I wasn't able to come back without any money.

DT: And that first night...what was that experience like?

Button: Very scary. There was a lot of girls who didn't know me, and when they don't know you, they tend to bully you and try to fight you. I also had other guys known as pimps harass me. One actually got close enough to me to grab me and try to take my phone, and it was just very dangerous and scary.

DT: How long did this go on for?

Button: I stayed there about six months, but a girlfriend I worked with on the streets knew I was getting beat up, and I was very unhappy, and she just told me she had a better place for me to go to. The guy she was with actually owned an apartment in Vegas, and it would be just inside the casinos where it would be more upscale and safer, so I decided to leave with her.

DT: Did this girl's pimp offer you the opportunity to move to Las Vegas?

Button: Yes.

DT: What did you do?

Button: I went to Vegas and the first couple of nights, I actually enjoyed it. Her and I worked inside the clubs a lot of the nights, and the hotels which were more upscale than what I was used to.

DT: Was the gentleman who had invited you there...did he really become your pimp or were you working just for yourself?

Button: He was my pimp. He did not let me keep any of my money at all.

DT: So, tell me how that works. That's very different than what we've seen here on the streets of Baltimore. You go into a casino...walk me through it.

Button: Well, you go into the casino and end up going to the bar. I was always sent out with $20, so I was able to put in the slot machine and I acted like I was playing. Then, guys would normally just come up and talk to me. You don't negotiate your price on the floor, because of the undercovers out there, and there's no entrapment law in Vegas. Once you talk to them and feel them out enough, I was able to take them to the room where we negotiate our prices and what we were going to do. And, once I was in the room, I would have to text my pimp the room number, the hotel, the amount of money, and how long I was going to be.

DT: Did the room belong to the guy you just met or would he just book a room?

Button: Correct.

DT: You were living in the apartment off the strip and then you were going to casinos...how many nights a week were you working? How much money were you making? How much money were you keeping? What was that life like?

Button: It was seven days a week from 8 o'clock at night 'til whenever I made a $1,000. I was not able to come home until I had at least $1,000 a night. And, he took all of it from me, and then anything I wanted...food, nails, clothes, I would have to ask him and he would have to drive me and pay for everything.

DT: My guess is that the average person who doesn't know anything about this life would say, "Button, why wouldn't you just walk away? Why did you keep doing this?"

Button: It's a mind game and brainwashing, and the pimp makes you believe that no one will love you, the police aren't there to help you because you do get arrested for what you do and if anyone finds out you do try to go to the police and go for help, you will get beat up and there's a million ways that they will be able to find you. I had a tracking device put into my cellphone, and my cellphone was linked to his bill where he could see everyone I was texting and calling.

DT: And the men who are hiring you, tell me about them. Who are these men? What are they like?

Button: I mean there is a variety...from college students to guys in their 80's, businessmen, car dealerships, landscaping, just all variety. Most of them were pretty nice to me, pretty respectful as far as my requirements and my guidelines. But there are some who do think since I am petite that they can push me over, and I've had almost called security on a couple of guys and screamed for help a couple of times.

DT: Did they end up running away?

Button: They end up letting me out of their hotel room, because they don't want to get kicked out of the hotel and have police get involved. Most of the men were there on business, so that kind of helped. They didn't want a big hassle and have their company find out what they were doing.

DT: So, how long were you doing this in Vegas?

Button: I was in Vegas altogether for four years. In the casinos, the term we use is freelancing. I was doing that for about one to one and a half years, and then I ended up going with an escort agency.

DT: And, is the pimp still controlling you even when you're with the escort agency?

Button: Yes.

DT: Tell me how that works. I don't understand how an escort agency works and how that's connected to a pimp.

Button: Well, the pimp would drive me to all of my calls, and it's just a way for him to keep me safer, so I'm not walking down the strip where the casinos are or just walking in the casino and hanging out there. Most casinos have facial recognition, so once I got in trouble and started getting arrested. If I just walk in there and I was noticed, I would go to jail. So to prevent that from happening, I signed up with the service to where they would just call my phone when they had a date for me, and they would tell me what casino what room number. Then my pimp would drive me to the escort call and then back to the agency.

DT: How much of that money would he keep for himself?

Button: The agency would get a base fee plus 20% of my tips and then everything else went to him, so it was like I was paying two people.

DT: Were there particular hotels you were called to most often.

Button: I would say the hotel I was at the most was the Paris Hotel.

DT: And, why do you think that was?

Button: The rooms were a pretty good rate, and it's in the middle of the strip, so a lot of conventions and businessmen. It was an accessible casino to everywhere.

DT: Okay. So, you're going through this for four years, and I know the manipulation is going on, but what's going on inside of your heart during all of this?

Button: Inside my heart, I was really torn. I haven't talked to my family almost the whole time, so I miss them a lot. In my head, I thought about them too, but I just felt so brainwashed that I kind of became one with my pimp to where I was so confused. I didn't know what I liked anymore. I couldn't decide what type of music or what food I would want to eat on my own, and it was scary.

DT: How many girls are experiencing this? Are you an anomaly or is this happening a lot in California or Nevada?

Button: In Nevada and California, there are a lot of girls...a lot. In Vegas alone, there's over a hundred and twenty escort services, and at least twenty girls per service on call a night.

DT: At some point, there was a crossroads. Did you want out? Did something happen with the pimp?

Button: I ended up going to New England to a strip club, and before I went to the strip club, I got into a big fight with my pimp, and he took my phone threw it against the wall. He tried to break my phone and tried to put his hands on me. I just had enough, and I remembered having black eyes a fractured nose before, and I was just scared that the next time I would have been beaten up would have been the last time. And I didn't want to end my life that way or living a life that would lead nowhere.

DT: And so, you're there in New England, he takes your phone away, what happened?

Button: He dropped me off at the strip club for the night, and he had another girl who went with me. She was keeping track of the dances I was doing and was texting him. So, I ended up going to the bar manager who got the regular manager, and I just explained to him what was going on. They put the other girl on stage while they snuck me out the back door and called me a taxi to the Greyhound station.

DT: I want to backtrack just a little bit. We're going to put the taxi on pause. Take me back to Vegas. Was there a time where you really felt like you were physically in danger at that point?

Button: I was. I actually got beat up by my pimp for three and a half hours. He fractured both my eye sockets, my nose, my lips were split. I had his shoe prints all over my rib cage, and at the time he was beating me up, I was on the floor crying. I was asking him to stop, and he wouldn't and I just remember praying to my grandpa who has – the one who passed away. And, I was just praying to him to just let me live through it, and I know I hurt my family and made bad choices.

And, the time I was praying, my pimp got off of me, because he got a phone call to go pick up some marijuana because he smoked. And at that point he got off of me, and he knew he couldn't take me in the car with him because of how bad I was beat up. And he took my phone and my ID and left and as soon as he left I was very lightheaded and dizzy, and I just tried to run as fast as I can to my neighbor to call the police and the ambulance.

They had a special unit common in Vegas called the Pandering Investigation Team, and they showed up. They took me to the hospital where I had contusions and just everything fractured. I had antibiotics, and they ended up taking me to a women's shelter and tried to protect me there until I was ready to testify. During the time of that court case, he actually got a hold of Ms. Jeanne (Allert) at The Samaritan Women, and they were ready to pay for my plane ticket to come to TSW. At the last minute, I got scared and ended leaving the shelter not getting on the airplane.

DT: Back to New England, you've had this experience where this woman is tracking your dances, she's up on stage, you sneak out the back door, you get in the taxi, where did you go? What did you do?

Button: I got in the taxi, and I went to a shelter in that area, because the Greyhound station wasn't open yet. It was raining and really cold outside. And the lady at the shelter told me I could sit there until my bus left. I only had enough money to get a Greyhound ticket, so I won't have enough for the taxi ride to the Greyhound. I ended up walking to the nearest gas station, it's about 11:00 o'clock at night with my stripper bag in my hand and just cash on me to try to put the money on my card. I was a couple of dollars short to actually put the money on, because there was a $10 fee.

I walked outside of the gas station, and this man who is very attractive ended up picking me up and he brought me to his house and he gave me the extra $50 and told me I could just sleep at his house until the Greyhound station was open and he would take me to the Greyhound station.

DT: Did he try to take advantage of you?

Button: No.

DT: Did you end up getting to the bus?

Button: The guy drove me to the Greyhound station, and I actually bought a Greyhound ticket for California. I had a best friend back in California who was willing to help me go back to school and get my life together because he was very mad about the path I went down.

My first stop was going to be in New York state. It was a two-hour layover because the Greyhound was going to take three days to get to California. But when I got to New York City, the port authority bus station, I ended up feeling really sick, my stomach was just very nauseous, I was just really tired and my body was shaking and to me it was just a sign of my body couldn't fight anymore the long battle I've been fighting within myself. And, I went to the nearest pay phone and ended up calling my parents.

DT: What did you say?

Button: Well, at first, no one answered the phone, and I was really sad. I left a message just letting them know I didn't have a cellphone, and I was at the bus station. I sat for a couple of minutes contemplating if I should call them back or if I should just wait and get on the next bus to California, but it took about five minutes to make my decision, I was going to try my parents one more time, and I ended up calling and my dad answered. He asked me where I was and I said I'm in New York City, I'm at the bus station.

And, he was kind of mad at me, he was like, "We haven't talked in a while, you know, you always ran back to us in the past when you had problems, so what's your plan? You just thought you'd come to New York and call us and we'd come get you." But, talking to my mom and my dad since I am their daughter, they didn't just want to leave me in the cold. So, they drove the entire way to pick me up with the pretense of knowing that I couldn't stay home, but I would need to go somewhere to get help.

DT: I'm assuming the ride home must have been kind of intense?

Button: My dad asked a couple of questions, but mostly he let me sleep back home. He was very happy to see me, but I lost a lot of weight since the last time he saw me, so it was kind of – he was very taken back on how skinny I looked to him.

DT: And so, you're back home, what were your next steps?

Button: The first step was I cleared out my purse of old phone numbers that were written down, I ripped up the Greyhound ticket to California. I got rid of some of my makeup, and I threw the stripper clothes I had out and the dress I wore to the strip club. Everything got thrown out, and I just came home with the clothes on my back. My dad got me a pair of pajama pants and his big sweatshirt and just told me I could go in my old bathroom and take a nice hot shower.

DT: Now you're at home and you have a conversation, you're sleeping, you're eating, what are the conversations or where are they leading to?

Button: They were just really happy that I was back home. And I'm an only child, so my parents couldn't handle everything, but they kind of knew what was going on. I actually wrote a journal to help them understand kind of where it started and how it led and what I've been through. And they actually read the journal, and my mom said it was a little intense, so we focused more on why I wanted to get in contact with Ms. Jeanne. I personally wanted the help this time instead of someone trying to push me.

DT: It sounds like in this journal were expressing that you wanted to come to The Samaritan Women...is that right?

Button: Yes.

DT: As you expressed that, how did you parents respond? What were the next steps?

Button: They were really happy, and they sat with me at the computer just because they didn't want me or know if I would get online and go back to old triggers. In the past when I was ready to come to TSW, I left at the last second. I e-mailed Ms. Jeanne, and I explained to her that I wanted the help. I was sorry that I didn't make it last year, and she e-mailed me back saying thank God she heard from me, and I was on her prayer board for a year.

DT: How soon did you end up coming here to Baltimore?

Button: I was home for about a week, and then I came to TSW.

DT: When you arrived here, what was it like? What were you feeling? What were you thinking?

Button: I was happy to be safe. I was kind of scared, because the house is really big and old looking, so I was kind of creeped out thinking it was haunted, but more so just relieved that I was not going to be harmed anymore by a pimp, that I wasn't going to have to do something that controlled my life. I was happy that it was going to start not just healing me, but also the relationship with my parents.

DT: And, since you've been at TSW, what have you been learning about yourself?

Button: I learned that I don't need a guy to define me or have me be accepted and loved. And I've learned that I have a creative side, which I never really knew or got the chance to explore before.

DT: What have been some of the experiences or events or services that you've really been drawn to, things that have impacted you?

Button: Volunteering every Friday at a soup kitchen. I really like serving other people and even if it's just to give them their only meal of the day. And just actually going to a Christian concert, that's when I really started to become closer and wanting to accept God back in my life.

DT: What would you want people to know...people who think that prostitutes choose this way of life? What would you say to the average person that thinks that? They drive by and they go, "Oh, she wants to do that."

Button: Not to judge a book by its cover and that us girls do not actually have a choice in it. We are brainwashed, victimized, kidnapped, forced into doing something that we don't want to do, and once you're sucked into it, it's not easy to walk away. Prostitution is no different than getting addicted to alcohol or a drug. It has the same effects.

DT: What are your hopes for the future?

Button: Well, right now, I'm starting to write my story, so my hope is within the next year to get it published and actually go and speak my story and tour different cities and states and go to college to get my counseling degree to help other women like me.

DT: What would you say about Jeanne and The Samaritan Women? What do you think about this home and what happens here?

Button: That I'm very blessed and I really do think that everyone here are my personal angels, and they are just here to help me heal. They have such tremendous hearts they give up everything to help rebuild my life, and it's just awesome.

DT: If you had the opportunity to speak to girls - 14, 15, 16 years old - who are thinking "oh, he's so cute" and they're on the verge of stripping for him - what would you say to them?

Button: If it's true love, he will not ask you to sell your body for money, and if it's true love, that he will find another way to provide and help and he will actually sacrifice something of his own instead of making you sacrifice your whole life.

DT: And then, one last question. If you had the opportunity to talk to people who are just learning about this issue and they want to help in some way, what would you say to them?

Button: To not judge us and if they see a girl on the street, to speak out, to call a hotline, or if you have kids just let them know to put Facebook on private, because Facebook is a big place where it starts with pimps and manipulation. And, just to let other people be aware that we are truly victims.

ROCKY

Sex Trafficking Survivor

After running away from home at 16, Rocky found that her drug use made her vulnerable to those who would seek to take advantage of her. While continuing to attend high school and living with friends, she began dancing at underground parties and selling herself to support her habit.

Lured in by false love, Rocky's newfound "boyfriend" coerced her to make money for him in strip clubs and eventually selling her on Backpage out of a hotel. While the stability of the situation created comfort for her, she experienced the harsh realities of violence and rape.

With the help of a detective, Rocky found her way to The Samaritan Women in Baltimore, and soon rekindled her love for baking, which I experienced firsthand as we talked in the kitchen. I was honored for her to let us in on her story during the early stages of healing.

DT: Talk to me about what life was like growing up. Did you grow up with both of your parents?

Rocky: Well, I did grow up with two parents. It was pretty normal until I hit probably around five or six, then my father just sat home and started eating his life away. That's just when everything changed.

DT: How did that personally impact you at five or six years old?

Rocky: It was just bad, you know, it's not what I was used to, so I don't know.

DT: As you were growing up, after age five or six, then what was life like? Did you keep going to school? Did you stay at home until you were 18? How did that all play out?

Rocky: Well, I went to school, but I couldn't really go outside. So it was like school and straight home. And, after my mother couldn't take living with my father anymore, then he moved out. That's when I was just – I was just acting out. I guess as a child and then I was in and out like – I was, well, yeah, running away and stuff like that until I just finally left when I was 16. I came back here and there, but it wasn't for more than like a month that I stayed.

DT: When you were sixteen and ran away from home, where did you go? What did you do?

Rocky: Friends. And I was still going to school, but I was mostly just hanging out, but that was it. That was my life.

DT: At what point during your season of hanging out or going to school did things kind of begin to take a turn for you?

Rocky: Well, when I got into drugs. I think I probably tried enough drugs for 20 people. That kind of made my decision for me, because it made me vulnerable to, you know, what other people wanted to do. That's when I got into dancing and, yeah, and I guess that's where it all started.

DT: Did you have a boyfriend who asked you to dance?

Rocky: No, it was just friends and, yeah, that's how I guess it started.

DT: You want to mix?

Rocky: Yeah. Okay. Hopefully it's not too loud.

DT: How much cream cheese do you need in your cheesecake usually?

Rocky: It depends, because in the pumpkin there's only two, but with the peanut butter, there's five.

DT: Whoa.

Rocky: And, yeah, and with the peppermint, no cream cheese, it's ricotta cheese. It really does depend, but like normally if you're just doing a regular plain cheesecake, probably from three to five. They're all laid out in my head.

DT: Have you ever tried a recipe?

Rocky: Yeah, I did at first, but it wouldn't really be Rocky's Cheesecakes if I followed somebody else's recipes, so I kind of made them my own.

DT: So...did you end up finishing high school?

Rocky: No.

DT: Tell me what you did instead of going to high school.

Rocky: I got my GED.

DT: Sweet.

Rocky: That was exciting. Yeah. Instead of going to school, I started working as a sales marketer, that didn't really work out. That's when I tried to get my GED the first time, but that didn't work out either. So, yeah, it was just mostly dancing honestly, and once I started going like to underground parties, that's when I started like really seeing that certain people, you know, do exist...like the guys if you know what I mean.

DT: When you're talking about dancing, are you talking about strip clubs? Or, are you talking about just going to parties?

Rocky: I did do strip clubs at first, but then I started doing underground, I started making more money, so…

DT: And, what were you doing at underground parties?

Rocky: Underground is not really mostly dancing. Dancing is just to get you a date. Instead of the strip clubs, you just dance, so somebody could just throw you money. With underground, you're really dancing to get a date, and it's much more easier. You can't get in trouble for it, it's faster and, yeah, I mean I won't say it's safer or cleaner, but there's more money there.

DT: And why did you begin to do that? Did somebody coerce you to do that or you just felt like you wanted to make more money?

Rocky: Yeah, it's for the money, and because I had a nasty habit of using, so it was to keep that up, honestly.

DT: And at any point, did you ever have a pimp over the course of time?

Rocky: Yeah.

DT: Tell me about him. How did you meet him?

Rocky: All right. Well, after I finished an underground party, I was with one of my – he was a good friend, but he was still a trick. We went to McDonald's, so he went in, and I guess he was around this area, so I guess he had friends inside and stuff like that. So, I'm doing my thing in the backseat, and then I stepped out to smoke cigarette. This guy pulls up in the drive thru. He's trying to talks me, hey, ma and all that stuff, and I have on my outfit still from the party and jumps out the car and he comes talk to me. So, you know, I don't remember exactly what was said because I was high, but, you know, it's basically like, you know, what you doing out here and stuff like that, you got a man. I'm like, no, I work, I dance and stuff like that. So, I know I asked him like are you – I know I asked him are you, you know, are you a pimp, and he said no.

We exchanged numbers and then, the next day, he wound up calling me and we met up and, you know, he told me that he was in the area and stuff like that. That's when he told me that he was a pimp that he wouldn't work me that he would just put me in a strip clubs. I didn't know like what to do in hotels and stuff like that. I didn't even know people do that. So, yeah, that's basically how I met him.

DT: Did he keep his word that he was just going to put you in strip clubs or did that change?

Rocky: Oh, no, that dream died down like the same day. I never saw another strip club. He put me with his bottom who was in the hotel who hated my guts. I don't know why she hated me so much, but she did. And, yeah, he put me with her, and once he found out that it wasn't working with her, then he put me by myself. I was just basically working out of the room and it's like since she hated me so much I hated her as much. It was basically, all right, well, "I'm going to make more money than her", so yeah, that's how that went.

DT: How are customers finding you? How are you getting your dates? Who are these people?

Rocky: It was off of Backpage, and they would call me. I had a phone, and we would just set it up like that.

DT: And who were these guys? Who was your average customer?

Rocky: Chinese and Mexicans kept coming to see me. One was, I didn't know what he did, but he was always in a suit. The other one, I don't know what he did, but I think he was a personal trainer or something. But, yeah, they always came to see me, and they were really nice. If I didn't want to do it like – because they saw how young-minded I was and how young I was, so they felt bad. But, at the end of the day, it's like, you know, what you pay for.

DT: How old were you?

Rocky: Old enough. I'm not going to talk about that, but, yeah.

DT: And, how long were you working with this man?

Rocky: I'm not saying that either.

DT: How did this begin to impact you differently than doing tricks on your own? How was it different? Was it better? Was it worse? Was it good? Was it bad? Was it scary? Was it awesome? Was it…?

Rocky: I mean it was, alright, it was good for the simple fact that I had some place stable, and he kind of kicked me off the drugs. Well, he didn't kick me off. He said, "I'll buy you drugs" and stuff like that, so, you know, he bought me them at first for the first week or two. Then afterwards he didn't have it, he's dry and all that stuff. So, that's how that happened. But, yeah, that was a good part about it because, you know, I had a stable place. I didn't have to worry about which party I'm going to hit. I just had to sit in a hotel room and do this. But, the flip side is, you know, I couldn't really talk to my family. I didn't talk to my family at all. I was always in the room trying to make a certain amount, you know, I'm getting beat like he always – at first, he didn't put his hands on me, but once his bottom left I guess I was just the bottom now, so that's when things got hard and stuff like that. So, I mean…

DT: You say "bottom", but bottom means what?

Rocky: You're the bottom bitch. When you're the bottom, it's like you have a certain amount of knowledge that no other girl has when they come in. You know you have responsibilities that no other – that no other girl will have. On top of that, you're closer to him than anybody else. You're supposed to be making the most money you know, you're supposed to – it's like you're on a higher pedestal than everybody else basically. And, it's like if other girls come in, if he's not around, you're in charge you know. So, it's not like there's a bunch of girls in the room and it's like, oh, well, who holds the money? And, the bottom will ultimately make the decisions if the pimp is not around. So, that was basically my position.

DT: Are you sleeping with the pimp simultaneously?

Rocky: Whenever he wants it, honestly like that's really how it went. And, depending on how involved you are with him, like, how much he sees that you care about him, is whether you deserve it or not. If you don't make a certain amount of money, he's not going to show you no attention. Mine knew how much I cared about him, so he used that to his advantage. "Go out there, you know, make me fifteen, however much you can make me and if it's a good amount, you know, we'll go out, we'll spend some time together." So, I mean, yeah, that's how it is.

DT: The average person could hear your story and think that you just wanted to be a prostitute before you even got involved with a pimp…?

Rocky: Okay. Well, I wouldn't say I wanted to be one at first, but when you care about somebody, you'll do anything for them. That's how I see it and that's exactly what I did. I did anything for him. And, most of the girls that are in the game, they're only in it because of the guy. He's promising her, because my guy promised me after a while, I'll give you a baby. He got three kids already, and I'm all excited because I'll be number four, you know, like that's the only reason why I stayed in it.

I started, because I was falling for him, and the work didn't really seem that bad, so why not? After awhile of me staying with him, it was just out of fear, because he used to beat me up like really bad to the point where I had to go to the hospital, but I couldn't. Most of the scars that I have are inside, and I'm not talking about spirituality. I mean scars that are inside, and they had to heal on their own and stuff like that.

DT: So, what happened next?

Rocky: I worked. I mean it's pretty boring, but that's all I did. I kind of got used to what I was doing, so I kind of accepted that it was going to be what I was going to do for the rest of my life, because I didn't see a way out.

DT: At what point did things start to change for you?

Rocky: Well, he got arrested. A girl that we picked up got him arrested, because she got locked up and she set him up, so she wouldn't have to do time, and he was put in jail. So, that's basically how it started – I started to transition out of the life. Once I went to one of his court dates, and they weren't letting him go. He was in jail for about six months, and I had to testify against him and stuff like that.

When he was released by accident, he got locked up again. This was during the summer, and now, he's facing – he's facing like over fifteen years. So, the only reason why I'm out is because he got arrested, so, yeah.

DT: Where did you go? When he went to jail, what happened?

Rocky: When he went to jail, I kept trying to hold him down, and send him money and stuff like that. But, I was getting robbed, you know, raped, and stuff like that. So, and I had his freaking – one of his partners like got enemies and stuff like that following me wherever I went. I was in Baltimore, but I ran back to New York and stayed down there for a little bit. But then I started blowing money too fast, and I went home. The detective that was in Virginia, she tried to help me out once, but I wasn't really with it after my court date. She tried to help me again, and then she sent me to place in the city. So, I stayed in the program like that, and then she put me here.

DT: Who brought you here to The Samaritan Women?

Rocky: The detective in Virginia. When I went to go testify, she helped me find somewhere to go, so I wouldn't have to go home.

DT: Were you excited to come here, or were you kicking and screaming?

Rocky: No, no, no, not at all, because after awhile I got used to not working. The first place that she put me in the Bronx was like, I don't really want to do this, but let me just try it. I tried it for a couple of months. I got there around the beginning of the summer, and I stayed there up until the time I came here. It was fine, like, there was nothing wrong with it, but I wanted better for myself. I felt like they weren't doing anything for me there, so I came here. I said I didn't want to be in New York anymore, because there was just too much going on.

After they got him arrested, you know, I figured I deserved better. She told me there was a place that was willing to accept me. I talked to Ms. Jeanne, and then I came here. So, it was a willing choice.

DT: So, when you showed up here at The Samaritan Women, what did you experience? What was it like? How was it helpful?

Rocky: I showed up, and it was different, but it is helpful because I don't have to keep in contact constantly with the people that I was talking to at the time. So, it's kind of forced me to move on, you know, which is a good thing, because I can't do it for myself.

They've given me an opportunity to do what I love. Never in a million years have I thought that, you know, like a program that I'm in or wherever I'm at - that I can actually be there and actually do what I like and have an escape. If I don't like somebody, all right, good, I won't like you. I'm going to the kitchen you know.

It's a really a breath of fresh air here, literally, and nobody can call me with problems or BS, I don't have to see anybody that I don't want to and, you know, I'm not forced to visit people or anything.

DT: Did you show up the first day and say, "Hey, I want to bake," or did it just come out through a class or a conversation or...?

Rocky: For the open house, Ms. Jeanne asked me what do you like to do? She knows I like to cook, I like origami, and she was like, "Okay, cool, do origami or knit sweaters or make jewelry." I didn't really like the jewelry, because I wasn't really good at it, so I don't like it. And, I wasn't really good at anything else. At first, I was just going to bake cookies and stuff like that, but, yeah, it was just going to be random stuff. But, then she put the idea in my head about Rocky's Cheesecakes, and then we just made it what it is now. I'm going to see how far I can take it.

DT: Why do you like baking? What's therapeutic about this for you?

Rocky: Well, it takes up time, and it really keeps me focused. I'm not bored for one and, you know, I'm not sitting down thinking about how negative my life is. It keeps my brain moving...it makes me make up the craziest cheesecakes to give to people. Making sure other people are happy for once – not for once, but it's like I'm thinking about other people you know. Trying to help other people in a positive way instead of, you know, rolling over, you know what I mean? Like it's different, and it's fun.

DT: Tell me what happened at the open house.

Rocky: Okay. So, we had a Samaritan Women open house, and I made cheesecakes. I wound up making over 35 orders that people wanted, and it went great.

DT: How are you feeling about this? You're saying that like, "Oh, they just ordered 35 cheesecakes." Were you excited? Were you pumped? Were you surprised?

Rocky: I was very surprised, and I'm probably still surprised because I can't believe that. I just can't believe it...it was just a simple open house I didn't have that much high hopes or standards I guess on how it would go.
So, I'm still really getting into the role of being a cheesecake maker you know. It's brand new to me. But I'm excited. I just don't show that much emotion so.

DT: What type of cheesecakes are you making? What's your favorite?

Rocky: I'm making peanut butter. I'm doing a peppermint. I'm doing a regular New York style, a Maraschino cherry, and dark chocolate one. I'm doing a banana nut and a pumpkin and a Ravens. My favorite would be the peanut butter, between the peanut butter and New York.

DT: Why is that?

Rocky: Because the peanut butter is good, but too much of it is like – try the peanut butter, you know, it's just too sweet for me, but the New York is pretty good, because you can have it with whatever toppings you want.

DT: Since coming to TSW, what have you learned about yourself?

Rocky: What have I learned? How much I don't like feelings. That and how sensitive I am to certain things or people. I don't know how to explain that one, but, yeah. And, a good thing that I learned about myself, I'm not sure, but, yeah, still learning, still feeling brand new to this.

DT: Beyond baking, do you love about The Samaritan Women? Or appreciate?

Rocky: How nice people are here. They're not all stuck up like they are genuinely here for you and want to see you succeed and, you know, staff is, you know, they're good staff, you know, they're not just doing it because it's their job, they're doing it because they care. And, the different type of people I get to meet. It's not just one variety. You meet people from different cultures from different backgrounds and from different beliefs. They give us opportunities to learn about ourselves plus God. You get in touch with God, and it really gives you time to work on you. You don't have much to really stress about unless, you know, you inflict that on yourself.

DT: If you think about the next six months or a year, what are your hopes for yourself?

Rocky: What do I hope for myself? That I don't get angry as much. That I deal with situations better...that definitely. You know, I guess gain some more knowledge by going to school or taking classes for culinary.

Another thing is probably branching out see if this picks up. That would be awesome. Or, you know, just being normal and fitting into, you know, society as someone normal instead of hiding from cops and stuff like that. That will be – that will be good.

DT: If you were able to talk to somebody who is seventeen or eighteen and thinking about starting to dance and thinking that might be a way to make some money or thinking that guy really likes them, what would you say to her?

Rocky: It's not worth it. You know she's so young – guys come and go. Just take a second – take at least a day to a week to really think about it or test him. See how much he cares about you. Just don't go off what he says. Really gain some proof, because if you're willing to go out and beyond for him, he needs to do something for you. If he really did care about you, you wouldn't be in a strip club, you know, you'll be behind the desk. He'll push you to go as far as you can, not as low as you can. So, yeah, that's what I would say.

DT: How about people who want to help, but they don't know how. They hear about this challenge – they hear about this issue, they want to do something. What would you say to them?

Rocky: You know you can't force it. You really can't, because it's just going to push the person away more. Probably like – if you know somebody, get to know the person on a friend level and then start to, you know, pull them away from it, but don't be that guy that's like, "No, you shouldn't be doing that." Be their friend, because nobody is just going to listen to another adult or whatever that's just telling them what to do.

DT: If you could say thank you or some words of appreciation to Ms. Jeanne or TSW, what would you say?

Rocky: Well, I would say thank you to Ms. Jeanne for being patient with me and understanding where I come from. The staff for not judging me, and really understanding each one of our wants and needs instead of just making like a general, you know, opinion about something and really taking the time to worry about each one of us as individuals and not a group. Yeah, really, Ms. Jeanne because if it wasn't for her, I wouldn't even have Rocky's Cheesecakes – thank you so much for giving me an opportunity for probably my last chance at life, you know, real life.

DT: All right. Thanks. I think I saw some emotion.

Rocky: Not that much.

BOBBIE MARK

Co-founder of Redeemed Ministries
Houston, TX

Having grown up in a conservative, Christian home, Bobbie Mark was challenged by her pastor to join a ministry with her husband to reach out to women working in strip clubs. From those initial encounters, she was propelled down a path that led to the founding of Redeemed Ministries and an aftercare home located on five acres just north of Houston.

With a vision for a 30-day shelter and multiple long-term aftercare homes, Bobbie is passionate about helping women experience holistic healing from the trauma of sex trafficking as well as the road that led them there.

DT: I'm just learning about you, and what you're doing so tell me about Houston. What's unique about Houston in regard to trafficking?

Bobbie: Houston is so close to the Mexican border, and we have an influx of traffic on the I-10 corridor, women are brought in through the borders all the time and we have money in Houston, big time. We have a lot of oil, we have a lot of business, we have a lot of commerce, and so that is just ripe ground for prostitution. We have gang activity in Houston. We have Mexican cartels, we have MS-13, we have all kinds of street gangs - Bloods and Crips. And we know when there's gang activity, there is going to be crime and so that includes prostitution and trafficking of course.

DT: Why would gangs be interested in sex trafficking as much as selling drugs?

Bobbie: You can sell a bag of cocaine once, right? But, you can sell a woman over and over each day. So many of the woman that we work with have been prostituted ten to twelve to fifteen times a day so they are seeing multiple clients. Once you sell a gun, once you sell a bag of drugs that's gone, but with women, you can sell them over and over.

DT: Tell me how you became aware of this issue.

Bobbie: Back in 2006, one of the pastors at our church approached my husband and said, "Hey, do you think you and Bobbie would be interested in doing outreach to strip clubs in Houston?" And, my husband knew my background. I was raised in a very conservative home and he's like, "No, there's no way she's going to go into a strip club."

We talked it over with our pastor, prayed about it, and then I said, "You know what? Let's just give it a try." And, so one night we went into the strip club, and we visited with a young girl who was eighteen. I was terrified that first night stepping foot in that strip club, but after I was there, then I was terrified to leave because I didn't want to leave these girls behind. You know I could see the pain and the heartbreak and everything going on in their lives. For about the next year and a half, we did outreach in the strip clubs in Houston just developing relationships with women, learning about their lives, learning about why they were there, what brought them there, their childhoods.

Along the way, we learned about trafficking, and we were shocked. I'd heard about trafficking in other countries, but I never heard about trafficking in the United States of America let alone in my own backyard, right? So, the more we learned about it, the more we knew if this was my daughter, I could not turn my back on her. With the ministry, we kind of shifted gears and focused completely on trafficking and started doing outreach in that area.

DT: When you shifted gears what are the things that you began to do? Was it more on prevention or education or did you have a vision for an after care home?

Bobbie: We didn't at that time. Our goal was to educate people, because if we didn't know, they didn't know. So let's educate people as much as we can, and let's do more outreach. In that shifting of gears, we stopped going to the strip clubs, and we started going to the spas in town. That's where we'd heard all the prostitution was taking place.

We just started taking gift bags with cosmetics, toiletries, hot chocolate, tea, and stuff - just going into the spas and just visiting with the women there. Sometimes, we couldn't get through the door and sometimes we were able to get through the door, and we did that for a while.

Along the way, we started to ask ourselves, "What happens if one of these women comes to us and self-identifies? What are we going to do with her?" There are no programs in existence in Houston for women who are coming out of prostitution specifically let alone sex trafficking.

We started talking to counselors and therapists. We started really looking deep into the issue to determine what it takes to help a woman who needs to get out of this industry. And, at that time, like I said there were no shelters, there were no homes, there were no programs. So, the first time the FBI contacted us with the victim, they called us and said, "We have a seventeen-year old girl who needs housing, she has no place to go, she's about to age out of the system, what can we do with her? Do you have any place?"

We said, "Well, we have our home."

And so, we opened our home and brought her into it. We had two teenage daughters at home at the time, and so we just brought her into our family and developed schedule for her and some programming. But, along that path, we realized that she needed to be with other women who had come from the same path that she had come down. She needed that kind of community to surround her so that she didn't feel alone that she didn't feel like nobody understood her. That's when we started looking to the future and realizing we need a safe home for these women.

DT: Tell us how many years ago the home opened. How many women have been through your program?

Bobbie: It has been a very quick process, because it was just a little over three years ago that we were able to open our first safe home in the Houston area just north of Houston with four beds. We have served twenty five, twenty six women in our home. Some have come for just a few weeks, some have come for a few months and we have a few now who are just getting ready to graduate at their one year point. We're really excited about that.

It's been a great process for us - a great learning process along the way, but we've been in existence now for about three and a half years.

DT: Tell me about their daily schedule. What do you do in the home? Is this holistic? Is it just to get here and hang out with whoever they want? Are there counselors? Is there physical, emotional, spiritual, and relational support? Tell me about the programming.

Bobbie: Our whole program is focused on four areas of healing. We consider ourselves to be a trauma-based approach to their healing which means the women are more important to us than the rules. So, we have a very strict set of rules, but we make adjustments to those rules as these women need for their healing.

Our healing process is a holistic one, so our entire programming is built around physical, relational, spiritual, and emotional healing. When we sit down and we work on our schedule, if it doesn't go back to one of those four areas of healing, then it doesn't have a place in our schedules.

We have a very tight schedule. Women are up in the morning exercising by 8:30, and breakfast is at 9:00. We have equine therapy, and so there's three times a week that we go to stables to the arena for the ladies to either clean stalls or work with the horses and receive riding lessons and participate in equine therapy and grooming the horses. They have coaster therapy, we have expressive art, and everything is scheduled from house cleaning to lunch to dinner, devotion time, quiet time. We have a "Fresh Start" curriculum that we're developing, and there's an hour a day that they spend in that curriculum. Everything goes right back to the holistic healing of physical, spiritual, emotional, or relational.

DT: Are there professional counselors that are involved in the process?

Bobbie: Yes, we bring counselors out to the house twice a week, and they are trained specifically with trafficking survivors in mind. They've taken additional counseling classes on trauma and a trauma-informed approach to the counseling, some different types of therapy, and therapeutic approaches that they use, but we do bring counselors out here and we often do group therapy as well.

DT: Do they work together to do chores and cooking their own food, or how do some of those practical things play out?

Bobbie: Well, our breakfast and lunch are basically on our own. So, there's a scheduled time slot, but everybody makes their own breakfast and everybody makes their own lunch. Dinner is family style, and we all eat breakfast together, and we eat lunch together, but it's just each person prepares their own meal.

For the evening meal, typically, the resident advisors will cook dinner, but sometimes the ladies have their favorite meals that they like to cook. And, there are times that they'll cook dinner at night, and there's times that the women will surprise us. We'll come in, and they've cooked dinner for us as a surprise and so, it's really nice. But, yeah, our meals are typically eaten together as a family.

DT: What are some of the challenges of opening a home? What are some of the ups and downs and twists and turns that you've experienced that you didn't anticipate?

Bobbie: Immediately, whenever we started the plans and the processes to opening this house, we're thinking, women are going to want to come here and they're going to love being in this program and they are going to want to heal and they're just going to be so excited, right?

So, we had these rose-colored glasses on obviously, and when the women began coming and we started learning more and more about the depth of their trauma and how deep the pain goes and how far back their abuse has gone. Many of these women are abused as children, and their trauma is deep. Then, it's not easy, because they often don't want to be in a program.

They come here, and it's a beautiful comfortable place, but often their comfort zone really is back with their trafficker or in an abusive situation. They're comfortable when they get frustrated with yelling, and we're trying to teach them how to communicate in a healthy way you. And so, lots of things we were not expecting. We were thinking, yes, it's going to be great and, you know, everybody is going to be happy and we'll sing Kumbaya [laughs] and it's not like that at all.

But, those are some of the difficulties and just the challenges and learning what do these women need to heal. And, what they need is for us to be consistent, and they need for us to not give up on them. Those are the things that they need. Some women come in, and they push every single button they can push, because they want us to give up on them because everybody in their life has. They want us to just kick them out of the program and just write them off forever, and then they can go about their lives saying, "Well, I tried that and it didn't work."

We don't give up on them even if a woman is dismissed from our house, she remains in our program, we work with her on an individual basis as an independent client of ours and we don't give up on them.

Some of the blessings we have encountered are when we get this joy of seeing women come to us and walk through our door completely broken and absolutely a mess, and then we get to watch them grow and heal and change and just kind of come into their own person and learn who they are. The first quarter when women are with us, the first quarter of their time here, we focus on "who am I" and that's our Fresh Start curriculum.

They're just learning who am I, what do I like to eat, what do I like to wear, where do I want to spend my vacation. And so, we get to watch them go through that exploration period and just learn who they are. And, it's really a joy to be able to see them come in as broken women and then leave so much better off in their healing process. They are so much further along and so we do get that joy.

The joy of sitting around the table playing games and hearing the laughter, the jokes, you know, just the way we poke fun at each other and just the joy that's in the house as we kind of become a family. Those are some of the blessings that we get to enjoy.

DT: That's beautiful. Talk to me about some of the other things that Redeemed does beyond the aftercare home.

Bobbie: We still do outreach, so we still go visit women at the brothels. We do some track outreach in the evenings where we'll go out and visit women on the track and do some outreach to them. We educate churches, businesses, communities, community leaders, law enforcements, schools. We've gone into schools and educated counselors about what to look for, some of the warning signs and so we do a lot of education.

We'll go to different community and civic groups and churches and do presentations just to educate them on trafficking 101. What that looks like and how can you get involved and what you can do to make a difference in your community.

Another thing that we're doing is we're in the process of opening up a 30-day emergency shelter. We found that average shelters just don't work for women who are coming out of trafficking and prostitution. So, we're in the process of finding a location and getting a 30-day shelter open which will act as an emergency location for them to become stabilized for us to assess their situation and determine what their needs are. Do they need drug intervention, do they need like suicide intervention, do they need a safe home? If they need a safe home, then do we have availability at our home or do we need to refer them to another organization in the country? So, that's something that's exciting we're in the process of doing.

DT: What are your future plans for the location where we are now?

Bobbie: We just moved into a 2,000 sq. ft. home out in the country, and so we're very excited about that. We have plenty of space and plenty of space to grow. So, we're sitting on five acres, and we are going to build a twelve-bed facility here on this five-acre property, and then we even have plans in the future to add smaller cottages on property to help women transition into the rest of their life, their next step.

DT: When you first met Ruth, what were your thoughts?

Bobbie: When she first came into our house, she didn't trust anybody, and she was very quiet and reserved and just really scared of her own shadow. And, it's been a real blessing to be able to walk with her as she uncovered some abuse in her past that she had covered up and pushed down so deep that she didn't even remember. And then to walk with her through that as she's discovering that and she's hurting through that and healing through that.

Then, to see her really fight to heal, it's wonderful because this woman is so intelligent. She's gone to college, and she is so intelligent and she has so many qualities. She's very peaceful, and she just loves animals and so, as she comes into the house and is just a lover of people and a lover of the animals, you know that just spreads out. It's just been a joy to be able to walk with her and see her come in and be able to grow through that and reach out to the other women as they come in - to offer them comfort and to help them get established.

DT: Tell me about Emma.

Bobbie: She called the trafficking hotline, and so she was referred to us. When we went and picked her up, she too had no trust. Of course, we have to earn that trust when they come to us. But, this woman has blossomed, and she is full of joy and laughter and she has such a resilience about her. She's been able to bounce back from this trafficking situation, and we've been able to see her and stay with her while she's crying broken-hearted about what has happened to her and been done to her and also frustrated and angry with her trafficker.

Then, to be able to turn around a few minutes later and to laugh about some situations, you know, and to be able to walk with her and to see her resilience has been amazing. She, too, is extremely intelligent. She has her degree, and she also has training in a very specified area and so, she has such potential when she leaves this house and get back into the job market and to follow her dreams and to make those come true.

DT: Okay. You grew up on a straight and narrow path, and you're now engaged in all kinds of stuff. You don't have to do this. You could be doing whatever you were doing before. What were you doing before?

Bobbie: I was actually working as an accounting person, on accounts payable. [laughs]

DT: You could be doing that. So, why are you doing this? Why are you leveraging your life in this way? This is so hard.

Bobbie: Yeah. You know, if these were my daughters out there, I would want someone to be doing this. I really would, and this is where I get a little emotional. But, the women come to us and some of these women have great family backgrounds. They come from all socio-economic, ethnic backgrounds, religious backgrounds. They come from all walks of life. The majority of them do not have families who care for them and love them and will support them.

It's really heartbreaking to know that there are thousands – hundreds of thousands of women out there and children who are being trafficked and really nobody cares. And so, if these were my children, I would want somebody to give a little bit of their time for them, and it's the least that I can do because I've been given so much. God has blessed me so much in my life that I have to give back. I don't have a choice but to do that.

And, as difficult as it is, they come in and, you know, sometimes they lie, they manipulate, take advantage of the system, but then to also be able to see the growth and the healing and the joy that comes from within and as they discover who they are, I just have to do it. Once I've lifted that rock, I can't put the rock back down. I have to do something about it.

DT: If you had the opportunity to talk to somebody who's just learning about this issue, what would you say to them? How would you call them to get involved? If it's pastor, an attorney, a business person, whoever it is...

Bobbie: Everybody can bring something to the table when it comes to this industry. Everything these women need for their recovery and for their redemption is sitting in the pews of our churches, it is sitting in the offices of our businesses, you know it is in our chamber of commerces. We need doctors, we need attorneys, we need dentists, we need counselors, we need mentors for the women, we need businesses to come alongside them and offer them second chance at jobs. These are the things that these women need for their redemption, for their fresh start in life. Anybody can bring something to the table. It doesn't matter who you are or what your background is, you can bring something to the table. That's what I would tell somebody.

Redeemed Ministries
Houston, TX
www.redeemedministries.com

The mission of Redeemed Ministries is to bring Christ's loving redemption and amazing liberation within our communities by providing environments conducive for holistic healing and guiding adult survivors of domestic sex trafficking to healthy, productive and independent living.

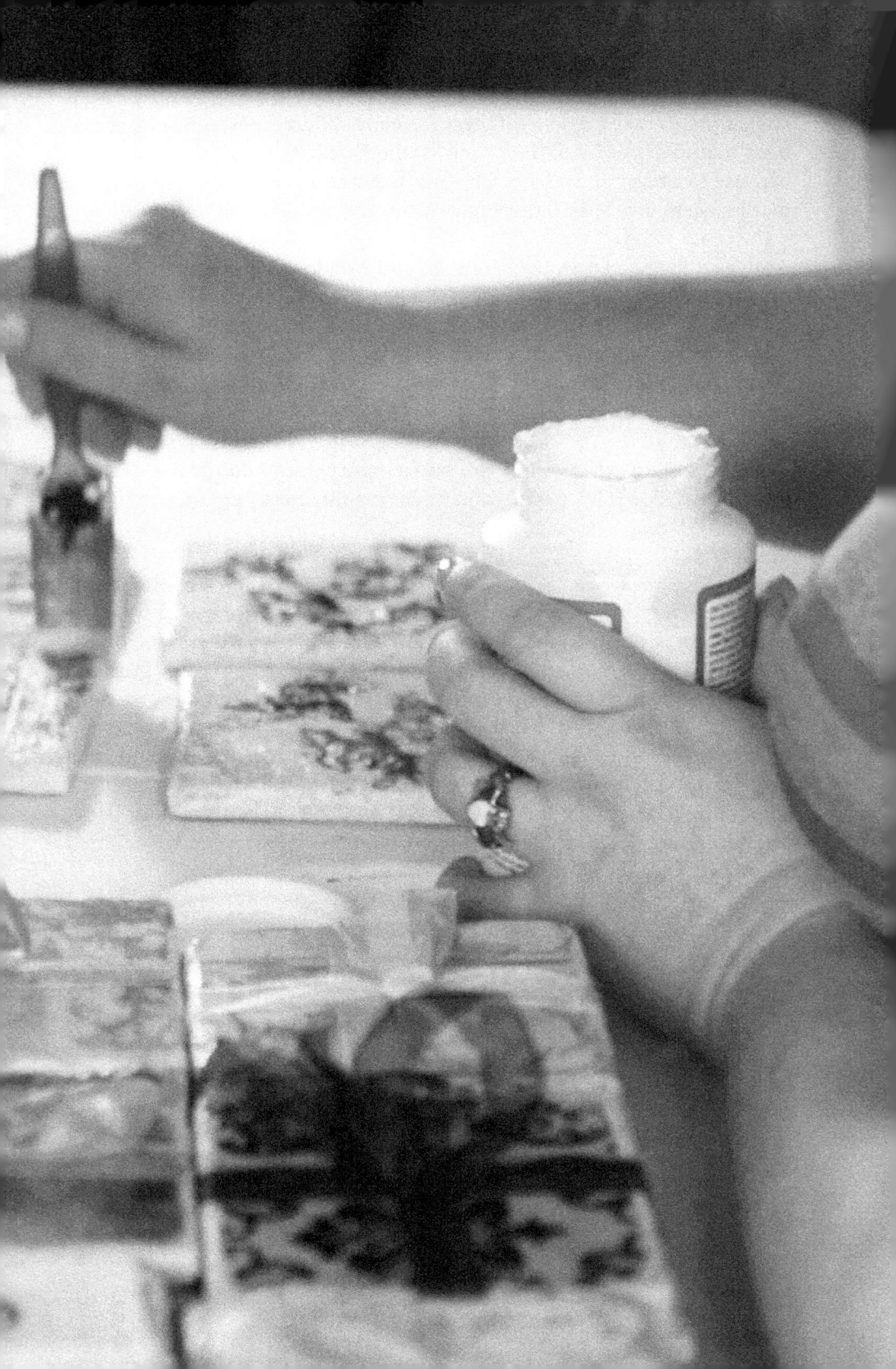

RUTH

Sex Trafficking Survivor

Surrounded by alcoholism and drug abuse, Ruth was molested by her mother's drug dealer as a child and eventually moved out at age 17. After a decade of challenging relationships, she was coerced to "do this so we can have a roof over our heads", but it soon turned into month after month of being sold online - including at the Super Bowl in New Orleans.

At a breaking point, Ruth reached out to Redeemed Ministries for help, and she's found healing from years of abuse. She's learning to love herself and allow others to love her while she's finding out that God has been with her all along.

DT: Take me back to your childhood. What was it like growing up?

Ruth: When I was four, my mother allowed me to be molested by her drug dealer. And then, growing up, she was an alcoholic and drug addict, so my life was very crazy, a lot of abuse, and I moved out when I was 17. And then, for about ten years, I was just in bad relationship after bad relationship. Guys introduced me to drugs, drug dealers. And then, I ended up getting engaged to one of them, and a week before we were supposed to be married, he ended up fracturing my skull and ruptured my eardrum and put me in the hospital.

And so, he went to jail, but I didn't want to testify against him in court, so I ran and then that's what brought me to Texas. After I came here, I was living in motels and just started running out of money and that's when I met him. And, he was fresh out of jail, so I don't know, I guess just wanting somebody there, and he said all the right things and really seemed like he cared. And he was like, well, you know, "If you can just do this so that we can have a roof over our heads and get a little bit of money, then I can start hustling and we'll be alright."

That one week and couple of times turned into several months, and he was very abusive. I've actually even had my wrist broken by him.

I guess you would say that I always worked the Internet, and so it was like you try to build relationships. You would have repeat customers, because it was easier that way just to have repeat customers.

I always kept in contact with a few of the tricks. And, this one particularly, he played a good game and talked a good talk, and he called me one day and said, "Do you want to go to Super Bowl or you want to go to New Orleans?"

And I thought, yeah, that would be cool, because it's Super Bowl time and it's Mardi Gras time. I've always wanted to go to Mardi Gras. And so, we went down there, and it turned out he is a pimp. The way I found that out is because we went and stayed with some friend of his, but then the next day after I realized what was going on I was like, "I want to leave," and he said, "You can't leave, this is your home now."

DT: So, you're in New Orleans. Has the Super Bowl happened yet?

Ruth: No, it's a couple of days before Super Bowl.

DT: So, it's a few days before the Super Bowl, and he tells you that you can't leave. What happened?

Ruth: He tells me I can't leave, and there are friends of his in the same hotel/motel and they had girls, too. One of the girls had gotten out of line and so, they forced me to watch her get beat just so that I would know not to try to get out of line and not to try to leave.

He would show off in front of his friends and forced me to do things with his friends in the room and - so then, he posted some fake ads up on the Internet, and then took me from New Orleans. We were in New Orleans like three or four days, but then when things got really crazy there because there was a lot of buzz going on because it was Super Bowl time, he took me back to Texas. And that's when my ex-pimp, the dude that I was living with, he finally realized what was going on, and he came and got me.

While he was coming to get me, he got pulled over and so the police got involved. And then, I went back with him, and that's how I actually originally came to get in touch with Redeemed. The detective called them and made a referral, because I wanted to get some testing done just because of things that had happened. And so, that was my first encounter with Redeemed.

That was in March of last year. And then, from March to May I stayed with my ex and things just got worst with him. From the time I was kidnapped to the time that I finally came to live at Redeemed, I woke up every day not knowing whether I was going to die that day. That was pretty much my breaking point. I just couldn't live like that anymore. I literally was getting beat every day. I was being humiliated every day. I was urinated on, I was just – it was crazy and I just couldn't do it anymore.

And so, I called them. I had been in touch with them throughout those three months, but I called and my intention was to ask if they could send me back to my home state. And, they talked to me into coming here and just giving it a try and so, I've been here since.

DT: When you came to Redeemed, what did you experience?

Ruth: When I came to Redeemed, it was pretty scary. There weren't any other girls in the house at that time. There wasn't anyone that I could go and say, "Hey, how do you feel about this? What is it really like?" But on the other hand, it was cool, because it was like I got that one-on-one attention that I needed.

And, it's been hard, because there's a lot of stuff back there that I've had to deal with and had to face that I never wanted to deal with and never wanted to face. I've run from things my whole life, so that I don't have to deal with them. I went from one thing to another. So, it's been hard, it's not been easy.

But, I'm so grateful, because I know that if it weren't for Bobbie and Natalie and Redeemed, then I wouldn't be here, I would be dead. I know that, because the beatings were that bad. And, if not by them, then by myself, because I was just tired. That's the true sense of tired is the way I was living. I was just tired.

DT: So, what are the good parts? What have you been learning about yourself and about life?

Ruth: I'm learning that I'm worth more than what I've had. I'm learning that even though I've had this rough life that God's been there the whole time. He hasn't deserted me. And, that was something that I could never understand before. If God really loves me, why is all this happening to me? Why did it start when I was four years old? Why did it start even before then when I was abandoned as a child because my real father left?

And, to me, that was just life, that was just what it was, but I'm learning that's not life and that's not the norm and that's not the way that it's supposed to be. And, I'm learning that it's okay to make mistakes, but it's okay to love myself, too, and it's okay to let people love me and it's okay to trust people because that's been one of the hardest things for me is trusting people.

DT: What do you think about Bobbie? Who is she? What do you think about her?

Ruth: Bobbie is a lifesaver. She won't stop. When I first met her, I straight out lied about my situation, but her and my case manager both knew that, and they didn't give up on me. They made provisions for me that they don't normally make - such as I was allowed to make coasters outside of the program when I was living with my trafficker. They rescued my dog, so that was good.

Bobbie has been a rock. She's got a lot going on, but she's still like that rock for you to go to. I feel really blessed because she and I were baptized together, so that's something that I'll always cherish. She's just really shown me that I don't have to live the life that I was living, and I can trust people. And, she's been there when I was skeptical, and she's been there when I'm like, okay, I can do this now, and they've given me chances and chances.

DT: What are your hopes and dreams for yourself for the future? You have a long, awesome life ahead of you. What do you hope for?

Ruth: I like interacting with people. Before I moved to Texas, I was in school to be a substance abuse counselor, and I still want to do that and make a program for women who have been down the roads I've been down.

DT: What would you say to someone who is just learning about this issue? What would have helped you along the way?

Ruth: Get educated, because a lot of people think that it's just something we choose, and it's not something that we choose. I didn't grow up going, "Oh, I just want to be a prostitute when I grow up." Don't be cynical to the girls. Just be a friend and be there and just show them love. That's one thing that I love about the RA couples here, because they show us that even if you've had a bad life before, you can still be happy and you can still have a true partner and you can still live a godly life. It doesn't have to be all bad for the rest of your life.

EMMA

Sex Trafficking Survivor

Despite having a college degree and working as a pharmacy tech, Emma was vulnerable to the schemes of a sex trafficker due to the brokenness of her youth. Rape, molestation, and a longing for love set her up to be lured in by a pimp who pretended to be her boyfriend.

What was supposed to be just a month in the game to help them "get a roof over their heads" soon turned in to over six years of being sold for sex. At a moment of desperation, Emma called her cousin who was referred to Redeemed Ministries.

Removed from the dangerous situation, she's rediscovering what it's like to stay sober, laugh, and experience true love.

DT: Talk to me about what life was like growing up.

Emma: My mom was a single mom, and I grew up in church my whole life. I didn't really catch on to God then, but I knew about God and Jesus and stuff. So, I did everything I was supposed to do in church. I went to church camps and to all that other stuff. And then, as I got older in high school, met this guy and lost my virginity when I was fifteen, and later on that same guy that I lost my virginity to raped me. And then, right after that my stepfather molested me. That's when my life started kind of changing.

I was still going to school, and then my senior year in high school I got with my child's father. We were together for about six years, and during that time, I had my daughter at eighteen. I got my Associate of Science degree as a pharmacy technician and did that for about six years or so. Then, that's when I met my "folks" - also known as my pimp.

I thought he was my boyfriend, and we were together before I got in the game for about six months. Then, it kept going on with him saying, "You don't want to live with your mom anymore, and you don't want to, you know, keep driving this car. If we do this, then we can get our own place, and then we can pay off your car and then we can do this." It was just this great fantasy. It's this great life that he painted for me.

DT: You're with a guy who you're assuming is your boyfriend. How did that conversation even come up?

Emma: I think we were talking about his kid's mom. One of his kid's moms was a prostitute and how he would be with her - how he would go with her when she was working and he was a pimp, that's what he was. You know he told me later on that he had been a pimp for like fifteen years. He grew up in the hood.

A couple of his aunts were prostitutes so that's what he grew up with. He's good friends with one of the well-known pimps in California, so that's what he grew up around.

DT: When he brought that up to you, what was your reaction?

Emma: At first, I didn't believe it, because I didn't want to believe it and then I was like, oh, he is not going to get me. That's not going to happen. So, I didn't think it would happen to me.

DT: What was the process that ended up leading you to get in the game?

Emma: Pretty much, my back was against the wall. I had bills and didn't want to live with my mom. He had a trust that he had gotten from his family - from his grandma and his mom. They had both passed away, and they gave him a trust and he said that he made a bad decision with his cousin. He had a conversation on the phone with a well-known drug dealer in another state. And, they had a conversation, so they froze his assets, so he has been dealing with that.

He showed me bank statements, he showed me papers that, you know, the DA is dealing with. He showed me all kinds of things to where it wasn't just like he was just telling me, he was showing me things. So, I was like, oh, okay.

Well, it was supposed to start off for a month. Then, he said, "I still haven't got it" - so it was another, "I need you to keep doing this for another couple of months." Then, I was like, well, if it's just a month, then I can just take a leave of absence from work, and then I can do this really quick for about a month, and then I can go back to work to keep my life going, but that didn't happen.

A year went by, two years went by, two and a half years went by, and then I got into a fight with one of his kid's mom. I left, and I was gone for 30 days, and during that 30 days, I got a job – a part-time job just to get me going. I just needed something to get my feet going. I got a place to live and got another car and just, you know, I was doing fine, and then he calls me. He's like, "I'm sorry. I love you" - blah, blah, blah, lip crap.

DT: Tell me what it's like during that six, seven years. What is it like to be in the game? Is it exciting? Is it something you want to do? Is it overwhelming? Is it scary? Tell me as somebody who doesn't have a clue.

Emma: It's all of it. It's exciting, because you see this quick flow of money coming to your hands. But, it's overwhelming, because you have to keep that up, and it's scary because you don't know who's coming to your door, you don't know. I worked the Internet the majority of the time, so I never knew who was coming through my door. I just knew what I knew on the phone. So, you know, it's everything. It's exciting, it's lonely, it's everything, - just about every type of emotion you can feel about something.

DT: Were you staying in one location, or were you going to multiple areas?

Emma: Within my six years – six and a half years, I worked in about six different states. So, I went from west coast to east coast back to west coast and mid also.

DT: What brought you the last location? What was the breaking point for you?

Emma: The whole time I was in Arizona - all I can think about was - there has to be more to my life than just this. I can't do this anymore. I was depressed, I was miserable, I was drinking every single day just to get me through the rest of the day. I'd be up, and then I'm like I can't do this anymore, and I'll start drinking. I shut my day down.

At prime time of everybody getting off of work, I'll just shut my day down, because I couldn't handle it anymore. I'd just start drinking. And then, I came to Texas, and I was almost raped in Texas. Obviously, it didn't happen, but my folks were extremely upset at me. I didn't know if I was going to get beat. I didn't know. I didn't know what he was going to do. For my punishment, since I hated working the track, I had to work the track, and I was out there for a couple of days. I would go in to my room if I couldn't get a trick to pay for an hourly. That's when I was able to take a quick shower, change my clothes, but I was right back out. When I was working in Texas, it was very long, because I was working the track and the Internet. I would be out all night, come in, take a quick shower, put my ad up on the Internet, and I couldn't go to sleep until noon. So, I had very little sleep, and I was tired. It was very, very exhausting.

DT: What was your breaking point when you reached out for help?

Emma: I was at a point where no matter how much money I brought in, no matter what I was doing, it wasn't enough. Everything I did was wrong, I left Texas and went back to California, but he had a friend that he was paying to watch me. And so, no matter what I did, I couldn't do anything right, and I knew it was just a matter of hours to where he was going to have his friend do something to me which I didn't know what it was, and I wasn't going to have that. So, no matter what, I just I had to leave. I didn't know what was going to happen. I called my cousin one day, and I just told her – I called her crying like I don't know what's going to happen to me. I don't know if I'm going to get beat. "I don't know what's going to happen, but I'm at this hotel and I'm in this room and I don't know what's going to happen." I called her frantic, because I didn't know. So, that was my breaking, because I didn't know what was going to happen.

DT: What happened next?

Emma: I called the 800 number, and then I was back and forth in contact with them through text messages and phone calls. My cousin was getting a hold of other places and trying to figure out how to get me out of Texas. So, she was recommended to Redeemed and told me to call. I called Redeemed and spoke with Bobbie, and I decided to make my decision to really come to the ministry and stay. Now I've been here seven and a half months. The beginning was crazy. I didn't know what to expect. I walked into the house, and I saw the other girls there and my first reaction was, "I would never be friends with these girls. There is nothing in the millions I would ever really just be friends with these girls." [laughs] And, you know, now we're best of friends like we're sisters. If it wasn't for me being at Redeemed, I don't know where I would be at right now. You know if I had to go back home within 30 days, I'd be back on the streets. If I had to go to a shelter, within a day or two I would have been back on the streets. If I wasn't here, I would be back on the streets no matter what.

DT: What have you been learning over the last six or seven months? What are the things you've been learning about yourself and about life?

Emma: I've learned a lot about myself - that I actually enjoy myself, I actually enjoy a life, I actually enjoy other people. Laughing again, knowing what it's like to stay sober and laugh - like joke with somebody. Learning how to love God and realizing everything He's done for me to this point.

DT: What have been some of the challenging things about being a part of this program?

Emma: Sharing a room. [laughs] That's a challenge for me sharing a room, sharing the bathroom. [laughs] Got to coordinate your times for everything. [laughs] That's tough for me personally.

DT: What do you think about Bobbie? Who is she? What has she done for you?

Emma: Bobbie is – she's awesome. She's done a lot for me - even things I don't know that she's done for me, and I couldn't ever, ever thank her enough or repay her. I couldn't ever do anything enough to let her know how much I appreciate everything she has done for me, because she's done so much. She's like another mom. She's taught me different recipes, because I always like to cook. She's done so much for me.

DT: What are your hopes and dreams for the future?

Emma: I just hope, honestly, I hope the best for myself. Right now, I'm in the process of trying to get my license back to be a pharmacy tech. I'm doing that and seeing if that's what I want to go back to. And then, just trying to get my feet underneath me and know what it's like to be on my own again. Just see where God leads me and see where I'm supposed to be in my life. That's all I can really do.

LOUISE ALLISON

Founder of Partners Against Trafficking Humans (P.A.T.H.)
Little Rock, AR

At 12 years old, Louise's step-dad started approaching her in an uncomfortable way, and she later found out that he was "grooming" her for something more. On her 14th birthday, he took advantage of her sexually, and she left the house vowing never to return.

After several years of being trafficked on the streets of Dallas and arrested for the last time, Louise was picked up by her mom and placed into a boarding school where she would graduate with honors. At 18, she returned to the gang who had previously trafficked her, and eventually she was purchased by a brothel owner who married her as his own.

After having kids, earning her nursing degree, and finding healing through Celebrate Recovery, Louise began to hear the term "sex trafficking" and discovered the need for an aftercare home for survivors in her own city.

DT: Where did you grow up, and what was life like for you?

Louise: I grew up in Dallas, and I had a wonderful family. I loved my family. I lived with my mom and my grandparents. My parents divorced when I was young, and at the age of fourteen, I ran away, and I was picked up a couple of blocks from my home. I spent the next two years on the streets being passed from one set of men to another. I was bought and sold. We were expected to bring in a certain amount of money, and we were frequently drugged.

They would put it in our tea or in our food, so I quit eating or drinking. We got to where when we were out on the streets, we would sneak into pizza restaurants and take the leftover pizza that people didn't eat. I don't remember changing clothes very much. I remember wearing the same set of clothes all the time. I remember being cold, and I remember being hungry. I don't remember a lot about it, blocked it out, I guess.

There was a time when one of the girls that I was frequently sent out with were in a car with four guys. We were typically kept on the inside of the care away from the door and windows, and the guys on the outside. This time, there were two guys in the front seat and two guys in the back seat with us, but we were put on the outside by the doors. When they came up to a busy intersection in Dallas, the guys in the back reached over us opening the doors at the same time and kicked us out right in the middle of traffic and pulled off. We jumped up, and we ran to the corner. We started brushing ourselves off and part of me was scared to death, because we didn't get any money. I was afraid of what was going to happen when we went back. We looked like and felt like trash, and we were scared.

The hardest thing about the time on the street was not necessarily being raped as much as the way people treated us. That day, when those guys kicked us out in the middle of the street, a woman drove past, rolled down her window, called us whores, and spit at us. That hurt a lot worse than the rapes.

The bad thing is - we could have left right then, but we didn't know how. Our minds had been twisted, and we believed we had to go back, and we did. I didn't even think about not going back. We just went back, and then we were sent out again. That's life on the streets. That's all the things that the women that we deal with have to live through.

DT: Take me into your mind as a twelve, thirteen, fourteen-year old. You said you didn't have any idea of running away at that point. I think most people would be astonished by that. How could you not think about running away?

Louise: You know - I don't remember exactly how I became so submissive to it, but I remember that we did exactly what we were told to do. When I first got there, I was moved into this one particular group, I was moved into the pimp's room, so I was in the bedroom with him. I was his property, and the other girls slept on the floor in the living room.

There was a part of me that hated that and I was afraid. Then, when a new girl came in, I was kicked out, and I ended up on the living room floor with the others and it was a nasty, dirty place with cockroaches. It was just nasty. Part of me was relieved that I was no longer in there with him, but there was a part of me that was jealous. We became a little bit competitive with one another, and at the same time we supported each other. It's kind of a strange thing.

They would make us go out at night, put on makeup, get ready and go out, and I hated that because I didn't want to wear makeup. I didn't want to look like a girl, I didn't want to put on the things that they told me to put on, the clothes they wanted me to wear. There were nights they left us out there. I remember nights being really, really cold, and I was by myself in the park and I would sleep under a bush. I slept in public bathroom one time, but they would always come and find me eventually and I would go back. I don't know why I didn't get out. I can't remember. I just remember a feeling that I didn't have an option.

I never even considered going to a shelter. I didn't know there were places to go, and I didn't consider calling the police. In fact, I was arrested a number of times. We were trained to lie about our age and given and alias and so I did and the other girls would come and bail us out. Only one time did I think of telling them who I was. Once a really nice policeman said, "Honey, I know you're not 21. How old are you, and what is your name really?" And I almost told him because I trusted him. But at that point, I trusted no one, so I wasn't going to tell anything about myself. That's when I became a very good liar.

DT: Why didn't you call your mom or grandparents?

Louise: I don't know. I have no idea why I never called. I loved my mom, I was very good friends with my mom, but I knew I didn't want to be at my house. My mom had remarried, and I didn't like my step-dad and that may have been what kept me from calling. He's the one who sexually assaulted me. She didn't know.

DT: How did you ultimately end up getting out of this situation?

Louise: Well, I was arrested for the last time at the age of sixteen. They found out who I really was and called my mom, and she came and picked me up. She knew I wasn't safe at home, so she took me to a boarding school, and I stayed there for two years. That's what really saved my life - just being off the street, and that was a place where I could relax and begin to heal a little bit. Being pimped out wasn't called human trafficking back then - I was just a runaway who was in trouble.

We didn't deal with the sexual abuse while I was there. We didn't deal with any of that. It was just a matter of getting me through school, which was good because I was able to make up four years of school in two years and graduate with honors. I felt confident, and I was away from the rapes. I was away from the drugs and the beatings and I felt confident that I had a chance to begin my life over again. And, the day I graduated I realized I didn't have plans or place to go and I went right back.

DT: When you say you went right back, what does that mean?

Louise: I went right back to the same nasty area that I had climbed out of two years earlier. I went back to the life, and I became a prostitute.

DT: Did a pimp recruit you, or did you choose to prostitute yourself?

Louise: I got back with the same gang. There were different girls of course, a lot of different girls, some underage girls and the same pimps, the same neighborhoods, the same people, the same buyers who were crazy, the same drugs, but that's what I went back to - because that was the familiar.

I was eighteen years old on the outside, but on the inside I was still that raped little fourteen-year old little girl that I had not dealt with, so that life was the only thing I knew.

DT: Ultimately, how did you end up getting out of the life and beginning a new path?

Louise: Well, I ended up getting married and then, I went back to school, got a degree and had a couple of kids.

DT: That's really fast-forwarding through life transformation. Help me out here. How are you making that transition?

Louise: I was working in a brothel, and another brothel owner bought our brothel and that owner did not want me being pimped out anymore. He didn't want me turning tricks anymore, so he took me as his bride and so, I married him, and then we had kids. He kept me out of the life. He was still pimping out women, and he still had massage parlors, but I stayed at home and had kids. After a few years, I went back to school and got a degree in nursing.

DT: When did you begin to hear about sex trafficking? And, as you became aware of that language, did you begin to put two and two together?

Louise: When I first moved to Little Rock about ten years ago, I was introduced to a Christ-centered recovery program called Celebrate Recovery and in that I began to meet other women that had been sexually exploited. Finding out that I was not the only one - and I know I wasn't the only one on the streets - but the lies that lived inside of me for years said, "You're not going to tell anybody this." I was shame-filled, I was guilt-ridden, I suffered from depression, I was suicidal.

The lies said, "You don't share that kind of stuff. This is about sex, people don't about sex. You are NOT going to tell people that this happened to you." I also believed that a lot of it was my fault. Maybe because I didn't leave, I was too scared to leave, but anyway the lies kept me really messed up.

When I began to come clean with my past, when my past came crashing into my present, I began to realize the things that had happened - then it started opening my eyes to things that were going on around me. I had ignored the girls out on the street. I always had a compassion for them and a love for them, but I had just closed my eyes to my past and I had not looked at that. And then, as I worked through my recovery, I began seeing what was going on around me. God was opening my eyes.

I was hearing the term sex trafficking and at this point, God said, "You know what? You've come through this stuff, you can help others who have been through it." And, I absolutely love my job.

DT: What were the steps that you took in order to become more educated and ultimately start P.A.T.H.?

Louise: I began to ask questions, talked with a lot of different law enforcement agents, and asked, "If this is going on in my area, how much is it going on? If there is any one thing that you need, what would that be?" And they said, "We need a place to put the girls. We need shelter. We can arrest them over and over again. We can do rescues, but it there's no safe place for them to go..."

What I'd heard was that in 24 hours they're back in the hands of their captors which horrified me, because I know what's that's like. I know what trap that is, and I know how horrible it is to feel like you're free for a minute and have to go back. Every time I was arrested, I felt like well, at least I'm away from him, but then I would have to go back.

I knew right away that I wanted to open a Safe House, and the minute we opened, we started getting calls. We also started a street ministry where we go out and talk to the girls. They hear about us on the street just to love on them right where they are. Many of our calls come from girls directly off the street where they get away and they call us and say I need help.

DT: Give me an overview of P.A.T.H. What is P.A.T.H.?

Louise: I would say that we're a victims' services agency. So, we provide shelter, a Christ-centered recovery program, individual and group therapy, life skills, and an educational assessment. We help them get caught up on life. There's a lot of girls like me. I was away from school from the age of fourteen until I went back at 16 to a boarding school. I had no life skills at all – at all! While other girls were learning how to have relationships, cook and clean and get a degree, I was just trying to survive, so I had no life skills. So, I think that's a huge piece of it. That's what we do.

DT: How many beds do you have? How many individuals do you help here?

Louise: We have nine beds here. We have found that the magical number is around five or six women in this particular facility. If we get more than that, there's all kind of drama. That's a lot of estrogen under one roof, so it becomes a little bit crazy. But, we can house up to nine women here.

DT: And, tell me about the program.

Louise: It is very structured during the day. They get up at a certain time and start with a Goals Group. It's baby goals just to get through the day. We have activities time twice a day. They have physical exercise every day, and crafts or another activity. They have scheduled, too. Two women take the meal planning for the day. They prepare the breakfast, lunch, and dinner for that day. A lot of our sexual assault victims have a problem with an eating disorder, so we keep just two in the kitchen at a time. That keeps them from grazing, because they have a tendency to gain a lot of weight and then they're mad about that. Their schedule is very packed Monday through Friday and includes recovery groups.

If they have a struggle with alcohol or drugs which a lot of them do, then we can go to an AA meeting outside of here. Otherwise, they go to Celebrate Recovery at a local church. Saturday is a little bit different. They do all their chores in the morning, they run errands in the afternoon, and Sunday is their day off. They get up, go to church, come back, take a nap, read, eat, whatever they want to do.

DT: In terms of your location, why is it undisclosed? Why do people not know where this is? Why don't you have a big sign out front advertising the need for community support?

Louise: A lot of our girls, when they first come to us, are scared to death that they're going to be found. They don't want to talk about what happened to them. They still cover up a lot of it with "it's my fault", but they're very afraid that their traffickers will find them.

So, we love our location. There are abandoned buildings and old buildings that are not used in Central Arkansas, and we love being in a building that nobody uses. The girls feel secure with that knowing that nobody knows where they are.

DT: Talk to me about some of the mental or emotional or relational challenges that the ladies experience. I believe you were mentioning that much of it points back to the time of their initial abuse.

Louise: The girls come in wanting to act like adults and perform like adults, but many stopped maturing when the assaults started. They have high expectations of themselves. Once they start talking about the assault and recognizing it wasn't their fault, they often need time to grow up all over, and their behavior is of that particular age. We see alot of temper tantrums.

So, we have a girl here whose first assault was at age three. We also have five-year olds, and seven-year olds - emotionally. So, they may be 21, they may be 35, but once they start going through that recovery process, going back and dealing with the sexual assault, they revert back to that age. Some of them hold their teddy bears when they talk, they play dolls, they slide up and down the hallways in their socks and laugh and they play – they even play dress up. One day, I was staying the night here and I came out and they all had capes on. They were 'flying' down the hall. They were playing dress up. And I love that!

It is so wonderful to see them being able to enjoy life and laugh and be kids, because that was taken away from so many of them at such an early age. I hate that they were robbed of that, and I love the chance they get to be kids here. They don't have to be grownups. We pay their bills, we feed them, we provide their clothes. They don't have to be responsible here. All they have to do is relax and heal and let us love on them, and I love that.

DT: How do you then prepare them for the future as you're helping them regain their childhood? How do you begin to prepare them to transition to being a responsible adult in the world outside of this caring bubble?

Louise: After they go through that healing process, they begin to hit a wall. They've done all the work they want to do, and they become restless. We watch for that. As they become restless, we begin giving them responsibilities. They can be responsible for keeping the calendar for the House or check the chores to make sure that everything was done correctly. Then, they either have to start volunteering or go back to school or get a job. Even if they just start out with volunteering, then they get a job afterwards.

But typically, about halfway through, once they start to hit that wall, they need to go ahead and get a job, and start saving – a part-time job and later full-time job or go to school full-time. Then, they're expected to save 80% of what they make to prepare for their exit from here.

We also have a "Rewards Room" where we take in donations of dishes, clothing, towels, furniture, and they earn rewards points with community service. And with that, they can start buying their furniture and their household goods and get ready for that first apartment because most of them don't have anything. When they come to us, they have nothing but the clothes they're wearing.

DT: Tell me some success stories. Tell me about ladies who have been here, healed, transitioned out.

Louise: We have one woman who came in at the age of about - I think she was 38 when she came to us. She had been sexually assaulted, had been pimped out a little bit, but went into business herself as a prostitute. After she started getting a little bit older, she began to hire her own girls, and she became a madam. And, she considered herself a businesswoman and told me that she could do nothing else. That's all she'd ever known. That's all she'd ever done.

When she came to us, she got off the drugs. She became a hotel manager and was able to graduate. She had never had a relationship outside of 'business' relationships. She did not have friends, and she never had a boyfriend. She began a relationship with a man, and it was very difficult for her because every time they argued she thought the relationship was over, and she began to crumble. While with P.A.T.H., she learned how to have relationships, how to love and how to be loved. She previously did not understand how to accept that love. After she graduated, she got married, had a baby and is working as a hotel manager. She's doing fabulous. We're very proud of her.

In fact, she even volunteers here. She comes back and works with the girls and gives them that hope and says, "This is where I was. I was one of you and I sold you" - and she gives them hope.

DT: Talk to people who live across America who are becoming aware that this is happening in their cities. What would you want them to do? How would you call them to take action?

Louise: I think it's multi-faceted. First, educate the traffick-aged victim on how to stay safe - especially in regards to social media. I don't think they have nay idea that once they hit that send button just how far that message or picture can go and how it can be used. I think we should help parents understand their responsibility and what they can do to keep their kids safe. In addition to that, I think to educate the schools and school counselors, school nurses, teachers to be aware of the signs of the student who suddenly either begins to withdraw or become hyper-sexualized. Something is going on there.

Also, I think society as a whole needs to look at prostitution differently. There is no girl who wants to become a prostitute. It's just not like that. And, we really didn't play with hooker Barbies when we were kids and say "that's what I want to be when I grow up." No, we wanted to be nurses or stewardesses or something else. Don't drive by prostitutes and look down at them and call them names and be hateful to them - but love them, pray for them.

Everybody can help in some way whether it's through prayer, financial support, or volunteering. Everyone can help in some way.

Selling people for sex is a profitable business right now. I would love for the purchasers to stop buying. I think that's wrong. If there's no buying of the product, people will quit trying to sell the product, so it would end the market. I'd like that!

DT: If you had the opportunity to speak to someone who is being trafficked right now, what would you say to him or her?

Louise: Oh, the first thing I would say is, "It's not your fault. You are beautifully and wonderfully made. Get out. Leave and go somewhere where somebody can love you and help you." I think we get caught in the mindset and the lies of "this is all you're worth." Everyone is worth more than that. Everyone's body and soul and mind is worth more than that.

DT: One last question. What is your vision for P.A.T.H.? What would you like to see five, ten years from now in the Little Rock area?

Louise: We're very small right now, but there's a huge group of women that need a place to go. My vision is to have a place where we can serve more women, women with children, and also minors - those under the age of 18 - a safe place for little girls to come. Also, a great community with a great reentry program, I think that's one of the main things - to get the kids get back into the mainstream of public school to get the adults back in the mainstream of the work force and to help them get that fresh start.

Partners Against Trafficking Humans (P.A.T.H.)
Little Rock, AR
www.pathsaves.org

P.A.T.H.'s mission is to provide safe housing and a program of restoration and reintegration for rescued victims of sex trafficking and prostitution, through a variety of services and Christ-centered recovery programs, offering hope for healing, personal growth and future success.

BARBARA

Sex Trafficking Survivor

After being neglected by her birth mother, Barbara endured years of sexual abuse in a foster home and was eventually adopted by a family who ultimately gave her back. A history of abuse combined with a slight developmental disability created a vulnerability in Barbara's life that attracted people who wanted to take advantage of her - including her own "step-sister."

Barbara found hope at P.A.T.H and began to experience healing, but she was triggered and eventually went back to being prostituted by her family. After growing weary of her old life, she returned to P.A.T.H. and started experiencing the love she's always longed for.

DT: Where did you grow up, and what was life like for you?

Barbara: Well, I was born in Memphis, Tennessee. My real mom had done drugs when she was pregnant with me and then after she had me, I was born with a hole on my heart, so they had to fix that. Then, when she brought me home from the hospital, which I was two weeks old, she had left me and my brothers at home by ourselves, but my older sister was there, but she's only twelve. And, she ran off with a man and left us at home all by ourselves and left me on the couch. I wouldn't stop crying and ran out of diapers. My real sister had to call DHS to come and get us.

When I was three years old until I was adopted, I was sexually abused by my foster dad. He would watch inappropriate stuff on TV in front of us, hit us, beat us. The foster mom would pinch me when we were walking or go somewhere and she would tell us when DHS comes to not say nothing to them, "If you do, you would not be able to eat for two weeks." And, it was very scary so I didn't say nothing, because I was afraid.

121

We only took baths on Sunday and weren't allowed to brush our teeth. I had to wear clothes that were too small for me. That man went to prison, and I was taken away from them. Then, I got adopted which was at the age of ten years old which I was happy. I acted up, because I didn't know how to control my anger because of all the stuff that I went through. And my brother, he didn't have very good behavior, and my adopted mom lied about him.

And so, she took him away and put him back in foster care. I missed him very much, because I wanted my brother because that was only thing that I had, because he was my real brother. I was sad that I didn't know how to deal with my anger, and because of the stuff that happened to me. And so, I started getting in trouble in school sort of writing letters that were not appropriate to boys and would talk about sex all the time, because I didn't know better. I didn't know you weren't supposed to – I thought it was okay to talk about that.

It got really bad with me and my adopted mom. She would over punish me instead of, you know, punish me and getting over it and tell me don't do it again. She would over punish me by having me standing in the corner like a flamingo and have me stand there until she told me to go the bathroom, to eat, or go to bed.

One day, I was so tired having my foot up and I went to go put it down, she told me, "Put that back up, your foot back up or I will spank you." And my foot was getting so tired, and so I put it down, she grabbed me, had a belt in her hand was spanking me. I turned around and grabbed that belt, and she grabbed the pillow. Even though she says she was trying to put it underneath my butt, she put it over my face was trying to suffocate me, and I kicked her as hard as I could.

I was in a lot of trouble and stuff. My adopted mom and my adopted dad got divorced when I was about eleven or twelve.

One day, I went over to his house because, you know, I went to his house for the weekends, and he tried touching me while I was going to bed. When I was laying in my bed, he asked me, "What are you doing?" and I said, "Nothing, trying to go to sleep."

He asked me again, and then he came over there and he told me to pull down my pants. I said, "Why, am I in trouble?"

And he said, "No," and he wanted to touch me.

I said, "No, you're my dad. Dads don't do that to their daughters."

And he said, "No, you're not my daughter."

And I said, "Yes, you adopted me. You don't do that, that's nasty…"

He was trying to touch me and I kicked him between the legs. That didn't work, so I punched him in his face, and then he left me alone and I told my mom. She didn't believe me, so she took me to the police station, and they said I was lying. I was sure I was not lying. They said I was nervous, and that I was lying. Well, who wouldn't be nervous?

That really had me upset, and so I just started doing stuff purposely to get myself in trouble - like I would stand in the corner and try to say I would commit suicide just to go to facilities because she had me in the corner all the time. She had me running around a tree and then she would say mean things to me like I brought her hell since the day she adopted me.

"You will end up making sex tapes, you're nothing but a whore, you're nothing but a whore, Barbara."

And it just hurt my feelings and I started believing it, and so I would make up excuses to get in a facility because that's where I felt loved. I'd bang my head on the wall and say I will commit suicide and so she would call people to come and get me to take me to a facility.

One time, I ran away from home. I was going to live underneath my aunt and uncle's daughter's bed with Cheetos. And, he ended up coming home and finding me underneath the bed which was obvious to see me and he said, "Barbara, get out underneath that bed." And he said, "I have to take you home."

I said, "No, let me stay here. I'll be good." And he said, "No, I have to, but I'll try to get custody," which that was a lie. So, I went home, and they ended up taking me to juvenile detention center. It was not a good place because there was a lot of girls that were trying to hurt me in the jail system and I had to tell them, "Please let me out, they're trying to hurt me and they thought I was crazy." And so they said, "Well, from now on you sit in the cell by yourself." I said, "That works for me."

After that, I went a long-term facility. I got back, she sent me to another facility and I didn't even do nothing. I just came home. I wanted to have a fresh start to work on things, because I had learned when I was there to try to work on a relationship with your mom. Well, as soon as I get home, I can't even say nothing, she tells me to pack my bag because you're going to another long term facility and I'm like, "What the heck?"

So, I packed my bags, and I was sad. Then, she was acting all nice to me in that one facility and I was like, "No, quit the bull crap. Just quit it." And then she wants to give me a hug. I just pushed my mom away because it was just a lie, lie, lie, lie. And so, she left and when I got out there, she told me, "Barbara, I'm putting you back in foster care. I cannot do this no more. You brought me hell, since the day I adopted you and especially she's like I have my own little daughter now." But, she's like, "You brought me hell since the day I adopted you." She's like, "I love you, but I can't take care of you no more, you're just too much trouble."

DT: How old were you when you went back into foster care?

Barbara: Well, at the age of sixteen is when – on my sixteenth birthday when I got out of that facility, she put me back in foster care. I was in one foster home, and the foster mom she was really sweet and kind of strict, but when her grand kids were there she would really let them get away. Like one of the grandchildren, which he had a disability which he knew better what he was doing, it was not a bad disability where he couldn't recognize what he was doing.

He would bite one of the other foster kids and we would go and tell her that. Then, she had him bite us again and say, "See, I know you're not lying now." And then, I just got out of control because that just made me mad, and I had temper tantrums.

DT: What does it feel like to go from having this family that had adopted you to now being placed back in foster care?

Barbara: I didn't feel loved. I felt like she was just adopting me, because she couldn't have no kids. Then, when she finally got a kid, she just pushed me away, and it hurt. I felt like a dog, her putting me away to be put to sleep.

When I was in foster care, when that was going on, it hurt my feelings, and I didn't let nobody come near me. I didn't even let nobody love me or nothing because I said if they loved me and wanted to adopt me, they were probably going to put me back. I didn't let that happen, so I had that thing going on where I did not let nobody love me.

DT: At what point did someone approach you about buying or selling sex?

Barbara: Well, after I graduated from high school, I started sleeping with men to find that love - without being paid. I was still young. But, when I was eighteen years old, I was staying the night with two of my friends at a motel here in Little Rock, They were supposed to take me to a job forum, and I walked outside because I was waiting for them to come and pick me up.

Then, these two women pulled up and was like, "Ma'am do you need something? Are you okay?"

Because I was like eighteen years old and I said, "Yeah, could I use your cellphone so I can call my friend? My friend is supposed to be picking my up." "

Well, we don't have a cellphone, but you can use our house phone." I said, "Oh, okay."

And so, I wasn't thinking. I'm thinking everybody is good and not going to harm you. I got in the car, and they drove to their – whoever's house that was, I don't even know if that was their house. And I said, "Well, can I use your house phone?" They started hitting on me and said, "We're going to make you prostitute, you're going to do all I say," and they pretty much dragged me into the car. I was kicking and screaming and crying and noticed people standing outside and said nothing. They did nothing.

And so, we went to the motel, they would set me up on Backpage. They would be sitting in their car every time I was going and turning tricks. They did that for three months. And then, one day I had finally gotten away, because they went to a trailer park. Then, one of the guys said, "Do you want to get out? Are you tired?" And I was like, "Yeah," because I don't want to live like this.

And so, one of his friends helped me climb over the fence. Then my stepsister started having me prostituting, sleeping with different men, and so I was on and off living with her. So, I would go back because I felt like no one loved me or cared about me, because she was playing mind games with me and making me think she loved me and cared about me.

And so, finally enough was enough. The last time I went back she started having me have sex with men – different men without no condom.

She had took me to one of the guys, and he had a disease and I told her, "No, I don't want to do that. He has – no, I don't want to do that."

And she said, "No, you go and sleep with him now." And she dragged me up in there and said, "She'll sleep with you – she'll sleep with you. You take her. " And then, I was crying.

Anyways, this one dude was wanting to do a role play of acting like he was robbing me and I told her, "No, I don't do that. Just tell him no." And she lied to me and told me, "He said, 'Oh, that's fine. I'll just…' – he just wants you to feed him and act like he's a baby."

So, I go up there and I knock on the door and he opens it, it's pitch-black dark, and then he's hiding behind the door, he grabs me, pushes me on the bed and I'm scared and he tied me up and just pretty much raping me.

And, I was like, "Please stop." And I started screaming and crying and then he put the duct tape over my mouth so I would shut up. And then, he turned me over and pretty much tied me up and was like, "I may do it in that butt hole."

I didn't want to, and I was screaming and crying, I said, "It hurts. Stop."

And he wouldn't stop and when he got done, I was shaking and all this stuff, and I said I'll just go home and I was crying like deeply crying and he told me to – "I'll pay you more," and I said, "No, I want to go home."

And then I thought about my stepsister. I should have be mad instead I was like, "Okay." And, I had to dress up as a nurse and he was spanking me with switches and I told him, "Please stop. Please stop. Please stop. It hurts. Please stop."

And, he just started laughing and said, "That's funny. You can take a hit." And then when I left I had – well, it don't matter how much I have. But, I left and stuff and this was like this is a shame and then I said, "Let's just go home. I'm tired." And, then I woke up at 7 o'clock in the morning from the van driver honking. I just wore the same clothes, left and I just couldn't live like this no more.

I went to my therapy place and told my group therapist that I needed to talk to my case manager. I told my case manager what was going on, and she brought the group therapist in and asked her does she know any places. She said, "Yeah, I know a place that she could go that would help her," and that was here at P.A.T.H. I was like, "Wow, I didn't know they have places for people that want to get off the streets." And so, she said, "Do you want to go? You know you probably can't have your phone." I said, "Oh, I don't care about the stupid phone. Have them come and pick me up."

So, she calls one of the ladies that was working here. Two ladies came and picked me up, and they took me to a doctor's appointment immediately. Then, they brought me here so I could take a bath, get some clothes – clean clothes on and when I came here I was like a little bit scared and I'm like, "So, was this the home?" And they were like, "Yeah. Yeah." I was like, "Oh, okay."

I took my shower, and so they fixed me a hot meal. Me and Ms. Louise talked, and then she told me I had a sexually transmitted disease which they got rid of. And then, I was here for four months doing good, doing what I was supposed to. I started having a closer relationship with God, and then all of a sudden, I was feeling angry about something that's really personal. I got really upset and mad about something and I just said I'm leaving. I said, "I'm leaving, I can't do this no more."

And then, instead of me talking to Ms. Louise and telling her what was going on why I was upset, I had my stuff packed and she said – because she knew I was coming back. She said, "Why don't you take only three outfits, and I'll bring it back to you, you just call me." And I said, "Okay." Got my phone and I left and I stayed with my – my stepsister picked me up, back to my ex-abuser.

But, I lied to Ms. Louise, and I told her my ex-abuser was not picking me up because I didn't want to hurt her. So, I went back to my stepsisters. She had me back to what I was doing. I was hoping something would be different, and I wouldn't have to do that.

One night I was working and stuff, and I made sure I brought my own protection. I told her I'm not doing that thing without no condom and I can't believe she actually said, "Oh, okay." And so, I turned tricks to help pay rent, because she told me, "In order for you to stay here, you had to pay rent." So, I gave her money around October and then around November 1st, she got me drunk and then my money when I came back I realized – I never spent that money because I already paid her rent money from doing things to get money.

I got tired of staying with her and stuff. I didn't want to be a prostitute. The funny thing about that is that God was telling me - He was talking to me in my sleep and He said, "Barbara, get up right now. Get up, go back to P.A.T.H."

And I said, "No, Lord they won't let me come back."

He said, "Yes, they will. Yes, they will."

And I said, "No, they won't."

Me and my stepsister went somewhere for the weekend, and something told me to look at the P.A.T.H. phone number. "So, I can call right now and let Ms. Louise know I'm doing okay."

When Monday came and I was back at home, I called Ms. Louise, I said, "Ms. Louise, I'm doing good, everything is fine. I'm going okay."

And she said, "Oh, that's good, Barbara."

And she said, "Come on back home. We miss you. We love you. I want you to come back."

And I said, "Well, let me pray about it."

And then I thought, "Hmm, I can do things on my own, I don't want to prostitute, so I'm moving back with my ex-boyfriend."

Well, I moved in with him, he didn't have me prostitute or nothing like that, but he was taking advantage of me by us sleeping together which is not of God and taking advantage of me by trying to get enough sex out of me, plus, trying to get me to give him money which I didn't do.

Then, he kicks me out, and he was threatening to take me back to my step-sister's house. I told him, "No, I don't want to go there." When he had the door open while he was driving on the interstate to take me back to my stepsister's house, I opened my door, and I was about to jump out and then he said, "I'm calling the police," and I said, "Okay, good."

I shut the door and the police come and I said, "I've been trying to tell him I want to go back to P.A.T.H. not to take me back to my stepsister. I don't want to go back to prostituting."

And he said I didn't say that and then the police were like, "Just take her where she wants to go."

I called Ms. Louise, and Ms. Louise answers the phone and I said, "Hey, I'm coming back to P.A.T.H."

My boyfriend wants to speak to her, I said, "Here you go. Hold on one second, Ms. Louise, he wants to talk to you." I'm thinking to get directions to meet her somewhere. So I handed him the phone and I'm looking out the window and then all of a sudden I hear him stop talking. So I turned around and I said, "What happened?"

He said, "Oh, she hang up on me. I guess she don't want you to come."

And I thought, "Well, what the heck?"

He took me back to the apartment and had my stepsister pick me up and I prostituted that night. When I came home about 5 o'clock in the morning, I was like, "I'm going to sleep for a little bit and then I'm going to call Ms. Louise and tell her I'm coming back. I want to see what's going on, some-thing tells me she didn't do that."

So, I called Ms. Louise. She said to me, "I didn't hang up on him. I do want you to come back. He hung up on me."

I said, "Oh. Would you come and pick me up? I'm at my sister's house. I'm going to act like I'm staying the night with whoever you're sending, I'm just going to stay the night you know."

So, I talked to one of the ladies that used to work here and was acting like I was going to stay the night, I had it all planned. I said, "Can I wash my clothes because I have dirty clothes?" and they were looking at me like, "What are you doing?" And she was like, "Yeah, sure."

She pulled up, and I got in the car, met Ms. Louise at a restaurant and then I came back here. I've been doing good. I just decided to leave that in the past, move forward because it had helped me to get all through this and I know that I'm worth more now and that I don't have to do that because they're never going to change. I might change, but they're not going to ever change unless God changes them.

DT: Now that you've been at P.A.T.H. for the second time, what do you like about P.A.T.H.? What has P.A.T.H. done for you?

Barbara: P.A.T.H. has drawn me closer to God. You know God loves you so much that He don't want you to be doing that to yourself and especially taught me to love myself that I shouldn't want to be sleeping around with different men and doing all that stuff, that I'm worth it and that there's man out there that like to play mind games with you to get you to do all that nasty work so they don't have to work.
And then, I love that it's a Christian-based program and I love that we can't have our cellphones, but we can use the staff or volunteer's phone and that's what I like about that.

And then, Ms. Louise and Lindsay and all the people that work here that are volunteer here, they're sweet and kind. We have our days, but they're sweet and loving and kind. And, but we have our own bedrooms and we get to take showers and we actually go and do stuff together as a family like go to church together as a family, sit together at church.

And we do family dinner. We cook together as a family most of the time. And then, we have people come in, and I love that we have people that come in that love us and care about us that do arts and crafts and painting with us, you just have to paint and sculpt, I mean I'm not a craft person, but I like to do it.

I love when it was Christmas and I got my Barbie dolls and coloring books and stuff like that for Christmas. I had an awesome Christmas and that's what I loved about it. People who love us, out of their hearts they went and bought us presents, and I never had a Christmas like that. And Ms. Louise would spend time with us - she was in her pajamas.

DT: Talk to me about the Barbie dolls and coloring books, why is that so special to you?

Barbara: Oh, I'm using the Barbie dolls like they're in the program like me for prostitution, so that when I get my own shelter because I want to stay here at P.A.T.H., but I would also want to go to college and be a Christian counselor. I want to stay here until I can get my own shelter and build it closer to P.A.T.H. and be on staff and work with girls with domestic violence and a drug rehab.

DT: What do you enjoy about coloring and playing with your Barbies?

Barbara: It's like my little daughter. I love her like – I love that little teddy bear. And I know it is a teddy bear, but still it's special to me because someone with a heart gave it to me and when I play with my Barbie dolls and stuff, I feel like a little kid, you know I'm doing it for – as a program and Ms. Louise plays with me also.

DT: Why do you like feeling like a kid?

Barbara: Because I have child spirit. I love kids. I want to have kids one day and, you know, get married and then have kids because I love kids and they're sweet and I like doing fun things with little kids like coloring with them and holding little babies and stuff like that.

DT: Tell me about Louise. How do you see her? What does she mean to you?

Barbara: She is like a mama to me that I never had. She loves me and she's sweet and nice and stuff, and she's very sweet and loving and kind to me.

DT: Why do you think that is?

Barbara: Because she's sweet and kind, and I see God in her. I don't see a hypocrite. I see actually a godly person that she has become, and I see that she cares about me and loves me and she has done a lot of things for me. She went looking and searching for me when I left here. Her and a lot of other people went searching for me. Someone that does not care about someone wouldn't do that.

My own adopted mom, when I was out there doing all that crazy stuff prostituting and stuff, she didn't even try to go find me. And, when I told her and she's like, "Oh, okay. Well, you can come stay here, but you have to pay rent." And it's like, you know I'm trying to get my own place, come on now.

DT: One last question. If you had the opportunity to speak to people who are not aware of this whole issue of sex trafficking, what would you say to those people?

Barbara: Well, I would first talk to people with disabilities, and I'd tell them how dangerous it is to take rides from anybody. It doesn't matter if you are trying to go all the way to the gas station and your car breaks down or well, or anything, you don't take a ride from a stranger. Or, if you're walking make sure you always have someone with you. Like me for instance, I was walking by myself one time to go to the laundromat to wash my clothes and dry them when I was staying with my ex-boyfriend, and a truck driver picked me, grabbed me, threw me in the back of his truck. He took me all the way to New Jersey, and pretty much was holding me hostage and was going to have me prostituting. I told him, "No, no, no." And then he took me, when we were coming back he said, "I'm taking you to California." I said, "Oh, no, no, no. I'm not going." So, and he had my phone, so when he fell asleep and stopped in Pennsylvania, I grabbed his phone and all of a sudden, "Oh, don't do it, don't do it." And someone saw me, "No, do it or you might not ever see it again." So, I snuck out and called for help and got away.

If you want to be in a relationship with someone, make sure they meet your friends first before anything. And plus, I would let them know how prostitution is dangerous. People don't care about you. They're just using you to make money, and you're pretty much like a tissue in a garbage can.

DT: If you had the opportunity to talk to people, families across America who are just learning about this issue, what would you say to them? How would you challenge them to take action?

Barbara: Pretty much watch what their daughter is doing, making sure they teach their daughters safety plans on what to do if they were walking by themselves, pretty much just teaching, explaining to their kids that it's not safe and that, you know, prostitution is very dangerous. People don't love you or care about you or if someone approaches you in the wrong way, tell them, "Leave me alone, or I'm calling the police."

LATONJA

Sex Trafficking Survivor

A pattern of abusive relationships was set in motion early in Latonja's life, and the resulting chaos caused her to long for peaceful place to seek refuge. In her mid-30's, she developed a relationship with a man who began drugging her food and selling her to customers. When she realized what was happening and confronted him about the situation, his violence escalated with no regard for the baby growing insider her.

After giving birth to her son, the violence didn't end. In fact, Latonja's boyfriend wanted her to turn tricks on the day she came home from the hospital after having a Cesarean section.

After becoming aware of P.A.T.H. at a local church, Latonja found the safety and security she had been seeking. For the first time in years, she could close the door to her bedroom and have a peaceful night of sleep.

DT: Tell me about your life as you were growing up.

Latonja: Well, I grew up in an abusive home with 13 other siblings. I am nine of the siblings – number nine. I was molested at the age of 4 or 5, really didn't understand what happened. Later on, at the age of seven and a half, I was molested again by a friend of my brothers. That was brought to my mother's attention which that was taken care of - which led me into a couple of other abusive relationships which I got out of, but the last relationship that I was in with my son's father was just totally different from the previous two.

It was hardcore abuse. I was beaten all over my body, hit with chairs, just for not wanting to either get high or prostitute and not have sex - that kind of thing. At one point, I would eat or drink, and I would notice after I ate or drink something I will start just passing out - not going to sleep, but just passing out. I'd blackout.

I'll be up one minute and just knock out the next minute, and I'm just up with no recollection of, you know, drinks or anything like that. And, just noticing different things going on with my body. Certain parts of my body that I had never allowed anybody to touch was being, you know, just a big difference.

With that, I stopped eating when he'd offered to fix me something to eat. In the beginning, I thought it was cute, "Oh, okay, you want to fix me dinner, you want to bring me something to drink. Oh, that's love. Okay. He cares about my way of being and he wants to make sure I'm eating I'm drinking - that I'm okay."

And with that, that's how he started slipping drugs into my drinks and my food. At one point, I didn't eat for a whole week, because I didn't know if anything else in the refrigerator had been poisoned or drugged. It just made me kind of nervous. I wouldn't eat or sleep, because I was scared if I went to sleep that, you know, something would happen or and don't know who's coming in - don't know who or what they're doing - that kind of thing.

I remember one night after we went out, we drove back, and he fixed me something to drink. I drunk it, went to sleep, woke up, and I could see my face lying face down. Woke up, I could see him, you know, from down the hallways pacing back and forth, but I'm feeling somebody on me, on top of me. And then, just hearing the sound of my body being ripped, I mean just literally being ripped, but not being able to feel it. That's how I knew then for sure.

I passed back out, and next thing I know I wake up and this guy is having sex with me and he's like, "Oh, thank you."

And I'm like, "What are you thanking me for?"

And, you know, and so I brought it to his attention, you know, I questioned him about it you know. "Oh, no you're just dreaming, you're just dreaming that happened."

I mean he's in denial all the time, but I know. It was degrading. It was one of the most horrible feelings to – for somebody to lure you and manipulate you as if they love you, they care about you when really you're more of a convenience. And, to just put your trust in that person or to even love somebody that could be so sadistic or demeaning and degrading is like one of the worst feelings.

It was hurtful and has led me to have trust issues. It's hard for me to sleep around people. I can't even set a drink down and walk off from it you know. I have to throw it out, because I don't know if somebody put something in it or not. Even though I know I'm around better people now, it causes a lot of fear. I can't even sleep. I can't get eight hours of sleep now. I can't even sleep past four hours, because I have trained my body to stay up all night and stay up all day - wait 'till I know he's going to be gone a long period of time just so I can get some sleep.

Going days without eating just because you don't know what's been done to the food or the water or anything. And, I had to wait until he'd go somewhere to actually buy something to eat if I had the money - try to save money and he found that, spent it, spent it on drugs.

I was in contact with other girls so he wanted to start using me to lure them in and to get them to start turning tricks. It was embarrassing for me, and it was hard. I didn't want to do it, but it took a lot of pressure off of me of not having to do it.

I mean there was a lot of times I witnessed girls out there getting beat down. I witnessed a girl getting shot. I got stabbed. He stabbed me one night. All this was going on while I was pregnant, confronting him about some things that his daughter had told me concerning him. Another lady he had jumped on her so bad that he almost killed her. So when I confronted him about it, he got offended and jumped on me.

I decided to fight back and defend myself so he ran in the kitchen, got a knife, and tried to stab me. Almost stabbed in the stomach, and I jumped and turned a certain way, so he stabbed me in the back of my leg. The blade of the knife was so long, it almost cut my rectum. There was blood everywhere - I mean it's just horrible. I was paralyzed in the back of my thigh. I had no feeling because a lot of damage was done to my nerves and stuff.

I'm just now being able to regain some feeling in the back of my thigh, so it's just horrible that he will get mad, get angry. This would turn into rage that's just like a blackout. I mean bust my face open just by punching me and just blood everywhere.

DT: You mentioned before we started the interview that you might as well start turning tricks after you realized he had been drugging you. How did you come to that decision?

Latonja: After I knew for sure he was drugging me - to just wake up and know somebody's on you and not being able to feel it, but hearing the sound of your body being ripped. At that point that's when I felt like, well, - because I don't know how long he had been doing it. And who the people were that were coming in and out. I'm thinking, well, I talked to such and such the other day, could he have been one of the people that came in and did something to me? People looking in your face and you don't know what they have done or if they did anything, so you begin to question everything and everybody, everybody's motives.

It confuses you a lot. It makes you not be able to trust, and so I felt like at that point not knowing and it's been happening, don't know how long it happen, I might as well go ahead and do it myself anyway.

DT: So, you begin to do tricks for him?

Latonja: At that point, I felt like I might as well just go ahead and give in and quit fighting him, because the more I fight him the worse the fights got, the more damaging they got to my body. So I decided, you know, okay, if I can't beat him, join him, so I did that.

Our thing will be we walk so far the street together. He's across the street or be so far in distance to where he could see me. And I'll walk up, somebody might drive by, speak. If they're interested, they'll either slow down and look, or they'll make a block and come back. So you slow down or I'll slow down and give him a signal like, "Yeah. Hi, what's up? How you doing?" that kind of thing, "Where are you going?" "Wow, you're trying to take me somewhere?" that kind of thing and go from there. Price is being discussed, what do you want to do, how you want to do it, you know, that type of thing.

We will have a certain spot that I would take him, and he would meet me there. I would get in the vehicle, and he made sure he got the license plate that kind of thing, so he could try to keep up with me. And direction, we always have a certain direction that we will have the cars and well, the people to go. And like I would say, I would go there and he would meet up. He will be standing either outside of the building, or he'll have a key to get in and I will make sure the lock is unlocked in case I have to call for him or something like that.

Most times, I would trick a person into going – getting so far here like, okay, this is going to happen, go ahead and get out of your clothes. Well, first, I need my money first, because you can always get your money back, but I can't get myself back once I gave it away. So, get the money, either slip it to him or hide it and in case I don't go through with it, you know, well, the money is gone. If he thinks that the person is going to, you know, jump on me or something like that, then he comes in, "Okay. Time is up. Man, you know, I live here. What's going on?" that kind of thing, you know, diversion.

And, we would do that a few times. A couple of times guys were kind of scary, because one guy acted like he was going to shoot me, but, you know, we resolved it. It's very scary because you don't know who has what if they carry a gun, knife, what they'll do, what they want to do, you know, how much money they're willing to lose.

It's just one big game, it's manipulation, a lot of deceit, a lot of lying. We got to the point to where he worked through the night time; robbing, stealing, robbing stores, Kroger's, Food Giant. I mean, go in and get rib eyes, New York strip steaks, stuff that cost over $20, you know that kind of meat. Take it, sell it, get the money, go buy drugs, do whatever. "Okay. I helped you out. I took care of you today. Are you going to do something for us?" So it's my time at night.

DT: When you finally came to a point where you wanted to get out, what did you do?

Latonja: Well, what happened was the police got called on a couple of incidents. I called them like two or three times. So, they were kind of familiar with the situation with me being pregnant, the abuse and stuff. They knew about the drugs. They had even warned me at one point, "Well, you're pregnant, you know you guys don't need to be doing drugs."

Anyway, I found out about P.A.T.H., because when I got stabbed and they were trying to give me help. They knew that he did it, but I wouldn't admit to it. I had to lie, and I promised him that I would tell that he did it just so that I can get medical attention. They were trying to offer me a safe haven, and they were trying to tell me about domestic violence places. But, I told them I would check into it, end up going right back to the same situation. More abuse occurred after that, and less than a week later, he jumped on me again.

A few more months passed by, and I'm having my baby a month early. Thank God he turned out, he was healthy fine. I couldn't bring my baby home because of domestic violence situation was so bad and the drugs. So, they let me stay at the hospital with him for like three and a half maybe four days. They came and talked to me, told me I could not take him back which I was scared. It worked out for the best, because I was wondering myself as far as what am I going to do if I had the baby and bring him home because I was scared that we might get into it – baby get hurt or even killed.

I was too ashamed to go back home, because I didn't want my family to find out. They knew something was wrong. We had some domestic violence, but they didn't know – they still don't know to this day exactly how bad it was. But, anyway I couldn't bring my baby home. DHS came in and talked to me, "You can't take him home because of domestic violence situation is bad. As long as you're with him, you can't have your baby. And so, we're going to give you a court date where we're going to give you a case manager, you call her, set appointment with her, and you guys talk things out, let them offer you help, and you decide whether or not you want to take the help. That way we can try and find you somewhere to go and that way you can work on getting yourself together and keep your baby."

I told them okay. I got out of the hospital. The first night I got out of hospital, I mean I had a Cesarean, he jumped on me the same night, picked me up and slammed me on the ground. He wanted me to go out and turn tricks. I wouldn't do it. I mean it was horrible.

Anyway, about a week later, the case manager and came over. I talked to her. He was there, he was present while she was there. So, just kind of gave him the runaround. Waited after she left and he finally, you know, walked off and went somewhere. I called her and told her, "I'm tired. I'm in a real bad situation here. The domestic violence is bad. I can't do it. I don't know where to go, because I'm not from Little Rock. I don't really know anybody. The only people I really know is the people the he introduced me to."

At first, she referred me to this other place, and I went there. It was okay. It just wasn't for me, because I was still leery. I had developed certain things about not wanting to be around a whole crowd of people and not being able to sleep. The people at that house go to First Assembly which knows about P.A.T.H. So, I met people from P.A.T.H. in a class. To me, that was a way for the Lord to lead me to P.A.T.H..

First time I talked to one of the ladies there, I was like, "They have a program for this?" like, "Yeah," I'm like, "Tell me about it." She told me about it. All the things she had to say was - you get your own room, well, like, "You get your own room. Okay follow me," you know give me the number. And so, I got the number, called P.A.T.H., and talked to them. I talked to them probably for about two, three weeks.

Thought about the whole process, knowing I need to get myself together, because even in growing up in abusive home, my mother still, that's one thing I love her for, she sent us to church. She tells us about God, so it was kind of like the prodigal son, you know going back home.

I swear it was like my safe haven. It was just like an exhale moment. I just felt at home.

DT: Why is that?

Latonja: Because it's like everything that I have been searching for that I lost. Just coming in to the door is like, "Okay, I found it." I got a chance to start over. All the services that they offer, I need it, I can do it. I mean I came in with my heart and my mind made up and I was tired, I was broken and withdrawn. I didn't talk to anybody, didn't want to get attached to anybody. Because every time I get attach to somebody, I mean there is that hurting. And if I wasn't being hurt, I'm being hurt so much I would turn around and hurt somebody.

DT: What was so special about getting your own room?

Latonja: It was like a safe haven. I just felt safe. Just me and God, and I can just close myself out to the world and pray and meditate and just be there to breathe and relax just find myself. Gather my thoughts, get myself together, and just enjoy not being out in the streets - not having to be three, four, five days at a time with no food and no sleep, no rest, just tired.

I could just come here and close my door and just lay there. I don't have to worry about anybody coming in if I did fall asleep. Anybody coming on top of me and doing whatever it is that they want to do - just having their way with you however they want to when they want to without you even having any consent. I just felt peace here. I felt love, the staff is great, and I just -- I just thank God for P.A.T.H. I thank God for Ms. Louise's dreams, because if it wasn't for her dream, her dreams have allowed me to get myself together - to be able to get back in a position to where I didn't fail myself or God.

Again, I recommitted my ways to God. I have mended the hurt, you know, the many relationship with my family, with my kid, and the people that I've hurt. I've forgiven the people that hurt me. Just finding new friends and family, people that want to have something and are doing something with their life. People serving God and just being able to get the counseling and stuff that I need - just being able to get help in every area. Just mentally, physically, spiritually, emotionally. I mean you can call them anytime, day or night, they're always there.

If she's not here at the facility, we can call and be like, "Ms. Louise, I'm having a problem with this" and she'll guide you through that. This is a wonderful program, and the ladies sometimes get along but sometimes we don't, but for the most part it's love, it's unity.

DT: Are these happy tears or sad tears?

Latonja: Happy. Just tears of relief - tears of joy - just tears of gratefulness. I'm just thrilled.

DT: Talk to me about your son.

Latonja: My little baby. I get to see him twice a week.

DT: Tell me about him. Tell me where he lives. Tell me what your hopes are for him.

Latonja: Well, right now, DHS has placed him with a lady. They normally don't allow you to meet the foster parent's mom, but I'm glad I got the chance to, because I was so concerned if he's going to be okay and is she taking care of him and I mean she's doing a great job with him. We take him to the doctor's appointments together.

We do different things with him together. We meet at the DHS office and, you know, we talk for a few minutes and I mean, he's always happy. I mean he gets so excited when he sees the both of us. He don't know which one to go to. He's just like, you know, look at me or look at her, and then he'll come to me, and then he'll look back at her. He doesn't want to disappoint her, but he don't want to disappoint me either. I mean he's so smart, he's just to love and just being able to be able to just see him and hold him and just thank God for him being okay, because I mean he's a tough little cookie.

All the stuff that he endured while I was pregnant with him, I mean all the fighting and being pushed into the edge of the counter. At one point, I thought we had killed him, because I didn't feel him move for four or five days. The drugs, the abuse, I mean couple of times he stood on my stomach, punched me in the stomach, hit me across the stomach with a chair. And just for him to just come out totally healthy.

I mean they've done extensive testing on him. Nothing's wrong with him. Actually, they say he's ahead of schedule, busybody, I mean smart, alert, and just looking at his eyes and just seeing the love and just being able to feel the love and just seeing the work of God and restoration.

DT: As you look to the future, what are your hopes for yourself and for your son?

Latonja: I want to give back to women who have been in my situation. I want to be able to reach out to them - let them know there are programs out there that could help you - especially this one. It's been a blessing to me overall. Since I've been here, we do community service projects, and I run into old people right down the street. They're amazed, they're shocked, "Oh, you're doing so much better, what encouraged you?" I mean, "You look good, you sound better." It made me feel good that they can see the change, you know, spiritual and physically.

They just let me know, okay, it's working. I'm doing what I need to be doing, where I need to be in this moment. The feeling of that, it just it makes me want to push on and tell women, "Okay. Well, I can help you or I can lead you to help. You don't have to take the abuse. You don't have to take the rapes. You don't have to take the manipulation. You don't have to accept the lies. You don't have to accept this lifestyle. You don't have to live like that. There's something better."

JENNY WILLIAMSON

Founder of Courage Worldwide
Sacramento, CA

After becoming aware that children are being sold for sex in the United States and even in her own city of Sacramento, Jenny had a sense that "her kids" were being raped and abused, and a solution soon became clear.

Surrounded by key stakeholders at the state capitol, she announced her plans to open an aftercare home for minors, and people took notice. After her photo appeared on the front page of the paper, over 200 people called her to join the effort. Six years later, Courage House sits on 52 acres, and she's getting ready to break ground on the second home - with a vision for many more.

DT: How did you become aware of sex trafficking?

Jenny: It was five years – oh, gosh, I guess six years ago now. I had never heard of the term human trafficking, and I never heard the term sex trafficking. I'm a mom with three boys, so girls don't really even cross my radar. And I was in church one Sunday. I go to church every Sunday because I'm a Christian, but I don't expect my life to change. But on that particular Sunday, there was a man there named Don Brewster, and Don and his wife, Bridget, went to Cambodia and opened a home for children rescued out of sex trafficking.

So, imagine my surprise when I expect my pastor to preach, and instead I heard this man start to tell me that I live in a world where children are sold for sex. And, he was telling about Cambodia, and he was telling about little girls and it – I don't know how to describe it except that everything stopped and everything got quiet and everything didn't make sense, but everything made sense at the same time.

And, it broke my heart, and I started sobbing, and I'm really not a crier and I started crying for these kids and for the fact that we live in a world where children are sold for sex. But, I'm thinking it's in Cambodia, it's in India, it's in Africa. And, I knew by my response that I was supposed to do something, so I thought I was supposed to write the big fat check. So, I wrote a check as big as would clear my bank thinking, whoa, I'm off the hook now, but I wasn't. So, for weeks, this knowledge stayed with me that I live in a world where children are sold for sex.

And the Lord begin to remind me that I always wanted daughters and I thought, "oh, I'm too old to have those kids" and He said, "Your kids are being raped, abused, and tortured on the street, those are your daughters."

And, I felt at that moment that in my heart got deposited this love for kids I didn't know, the daughters that I always wanted and the fact that as a mother I now knew that my children are being sold for sex. But I'm still thinking, I'm going to Cambodia now and I'm trying to figure out how to tell my husband that I'm leaving and going to Cambodia until I started doing research on the Internet.

I put in the words "human trafficking", and I put in the words "sex trafficking", and Sacramento came up on my computer, of all the searches, Sacramento. I started reading the report that they've done in California that California is the number one state in trafficking from all of our borders and our ports. And I read on and on and on about the problem and how big it was and the problem of how big it was, and then there were these sentences that said, but there are no homes or services. And, they jumped out at me. I'm really logical person and I was like, okay, we know the problem and we know the solution, let's just build a home and it was that simple in my mind. We'll just build a home.

I already had a non-profit organization. I'm a life coach. I do Courage conferences to help people find their purpose and I just felt like, you know what? These kids have a purpose, they were created for something, so let's build a home and create an environment where they can figure out who they are and what they're supposed to be doing and so, it was that simple, we'll build homes.

DT: As you came to that conclusion, what are the tangible steps that you took in order to open Courage House?

Jenny: Well, first I became an expert on the issue, and I tell people that all the time. If this issue breaks your heart or whatever issue breaks your heart, know the details, know what's happening, find the facts the figure, don't just be broken-hearted over it.

I think that's what happened to me. When I heard I live in a world where children were sold for sex and my heart was broken, that paralyzed me. When I found out it was happening in my own backyard, I got pissed off.

And so, it's like everything changed from, oh, my God this is so big and it's so horrible to, wait, wait, wait, in my own backyard? And now it had a different feeling to it.

So, I did research, I studied anything I could, I read every word in the state of California report and then, one day I pick the phone up and I called the author of the state of California Report. Her name was Nancy Matheson.

I actually got to meet her one day and I said, "Hello," in my most professional voice, "My name is Jenny Williamson. I have a non-profit organization. I see that there's a huge human trafficking issue in the state of California, and my organization would like to build a home to house these children."

And she goes, "Really? We're having a meeting tomorrow, would you like to come?"

And then, I freaked out, "Oh, my God I'm going to the capitol."

And, I went to the meeting at the state capitol and I listened to people again talk about the problem, and I'm shocked because I just found out, but there are people who know. They know our children are being trafficked right now. They know it, but there's no homes and services. I thought in this day and age in our time of history, if there's a problem, we've got the solution whether it's the government or the church or somebody. I'm still in shock that there's no homes and services, but we know about the problem.

So, I sat at the meeting, and I listened. I wasn't going to talk, because I knew I was in the room with people way smarter than me. But after about two and a half hours of listening to the problem, I just stood up and said, "My non-profit organization will build a home." I have absolutely no idea what that means, I have no money, I don't even know how to get kids in a home, but I just announced it.

And then, I left, and I cried all the way home because I figured I embarrass myself and sounded like an idiot. And then I made another phone call and I called the police department and I said, "Do we really have a problem here with children being trafficked?" And they were like, "Absolutely. We're having a meeting tomorrow, want to come?" And I'm freaking out because people are believing me, they're like taking me seriously, and I still didn't even know what this all means.

I went down to the juvenile department, the police department and they introduced me to the FBI, they offered for me to be able to go on ride-alongs. They literally educated me on the problem in Sacramento. And this problem has so many faces across the United States, but in our city in Sacramento, they already had a task force that was rescuing kids and what the FBI agent said to me was so profound, "We were given this mandate from the federal government to look for kids and put away bad guys, but nobody asked the question where are we going to put the kids."

So, he said, "We were left to what we had always done was either take them to the children's receiving center where they jump the fence and run, take them back home to the situation where they just ran from, or lock them up in juvenile hall. And that's what we were left with is lock in juvenile hall, but we don't have a place to put them after that." So, once again I said, "My organization is going to build a home." And they were two phone calls that literally changed my life.

DT: Talk to me about the uniqueness of Sacramento and how trafficking uniquely plays out for minors.

Jenny: What I found out is that about 90-95% of the kids that they were picking up, I really can't speak to the problems because nobody knows, it's done in secret, so, you know, we're just summarizing. But what the FBI said from the kids they're picking up, large percentage of them were already in the foster care system.

Our particular situation is that we've got the intersecting of highways. So, in the state of California, you've got Interstate 5, you've got Interstate 80, the highways crossing and so Sacramento is like a hub. You're going up to Seattle, and then you're going over to Las Vegas and so it's like we all converge here. So there's a lot of trafficking happening up and down the highways, but the FBI said the majority are local girls. What we're finding with our Sacramento girls is they'll find our girls in Las Vegas, they'll find our girls in Reno, they'll find our girls in L.A., in San Diego, but our girls are pretty much local.

And so, the average age is thirteen or fourteen getting into this. Most of them have very dysfunctional families that just haven't been able, for a number of reasons, to keep them safe, and they think that this is their only option.

I tell people all the time, you and I are shocked by the issue of trafficking, but what was shocking to most of our kids is that they were abused physically and sexually at very young ages. So, the commercial trafficking, being prostituted, by now they believe that's all that they're made for. That's not as shocking to them as it is you and I.

DT: Take us briefly through the process of raising the finances and opening the aftercare home for minors.

Jenny: Picking up the phone was the easy part. The two phone calls and then I went to my church, and I took the FBI agent with me who had been rescuing girls because I didn't know about trafficking, so I didn't assume anybody else would. I figured if the FBI tells you there's a problem, then you'd believe them. But, they probably just think I was crazy.

And so, I took the FBI agent with me to my church and I said, "We live in a world where children is sold for sex and it's happening right here in our own backyard. " And you could just see the shocked look on their faces. The missions pastor is like, "I don't know what to do about this." Missions is far away, right?

And then, I took the FBI officer with me to more churches all around the city, and there was that same blank paralyzed look like, okay, what do you want us to do about it. It's so big, churches aren't in the business of opening a home, you know, outside of their doors. And so, I just started telling people that it was our responsibility.

And again, you have to go back to, I'm now a mom who believes her daughters are missing. I'm now a mom who is shamelessly begging anybody to help me find my kids, because now that I have this knowledge I can't sleep at night. Now that I have this knowledge, I'm just imagining my own child. What would you do? You wouldn't go to work, you would shamelessly beg people for money, you would do whatever it took and that's what it feels like to me inside - this is my kid.

And so, I went to the place that I knew, which is the church, because I believe it is their responsibility. In the beginning, they had budgets, and they had two-year plans, and this wasn't in their plan. And so, the original couple I told you about from Cambodia, I called them when they were back in the States and basically fell down and cried in their laps going, "Oh, my God, how do you do this? How do you do this big huge enormous dream? How do you live? What did you do?"

They sold everything they had and moved to Cambodia and I was like, "Oh, yeah, I don't have to do that. I could stay here."

But, they just said "one step at a time." And so, that really is a series of steps, but on that day, the newspaper, our local newspaper, The Sacramento Bee, happened to be there interviewing them, and Bridget Brewster announced to the reporter that this is Jenny Williamson and she has an organization, and she's going to build a home just like ours here in Sacramento.

They started taking pictures of me and they interviewed me and they asked for my business phone number, which I didn't have, so I gave my home phone number.

The next morning at 5:00 AM, the phone starts ringing, I'm on the front page of the newspaper and over 200 people called and e-mailed and said, "We're in. We will help you build a home." And that is how it all kind of began. And on that day, when I had those 200 phone calls, I had three women who called me and they also said the exact same thing to me. They identified themselves as a prostitute, not my word, theirs and they said, "Please build a home, there wasn't one when we were little. And we see young girls out on the streets and we don't want them to be like us. They just need someone to believe in them."

The exact words, "They just need someone to believe in them."

And so, on that day when I was in the paper, my FBI agent called me and said, "Hey, I want you to come and meet a fifteen-year old." And I said, "No." I refused to meet any of the kids. When somebody has no hope and you just say, "Oh, I'm going to build a home. Hang on." I just – I didn't want to do it, I was afraid I would take them all with me, because I'm a mom. These are my kids.

And so, when the FBI agent tells you to come, you go. So, I said, "Okay." I went and had lunch and I met this fifteen-year old, and I told this dream of a place with a lot of open spaces that could be their home. It was the biggest dream. And she said I just need somebody to believe in me. So, again these words stayed with me for days and days, believe in me. Who would I be if you believe in me?

I started saying, "Oh my gosh, we need a song. We need a video." How are we going to tell the story to the church people? How do you show up on Sunday morning saying let's talk about sex. Well, not just sex, but let's talk about children being sold. Everybody's like, no, thank you, that's not what we come to church for.

And so, one of those 200 phone calls was a woman who's a local woman and a songwriter, and I was writing doodling on a piece of paper if you will and she's like, "What are you doing?" I go, "There's a song in my head, I'm not a songwriter that says who would I be if you believe in me." And she said, "Well, I'm a songwriter," and she wrote this song.

And long story, this young man came, and said he's a film maker and somebody raised a bunch of money, and we made this video called, Believe In Me to help tell the story of these girls. And with that video and with the local churches, we had local musicians start writing songs for us, put together a CD, and we started doing concerts and that is how we raised almost a million dollars to open a home here in California and in Tanzania, Africa with music and with the Believe In Me video.

DT: Tell us about Courage House. What is it like?

Jenny: In my mind, it was a dream where there's wide-open spaces and there is mountains and hills and creeks and with picket fences and horses. And so, when I saw the property, it was what I saw in my mind. And so, because I did all of that research in the beginning and tried to understand this population this kid, what were they going to need, what can we do, what can't we do, what's the best practices. And there just wasn't a lot out there at the time, because there weren't that many homes, there were just three in the United States at the time when we opened Courage House and so, there wasn't a lot to pull from.

I found out that most of our kids if they were in foster care system, they miss a lot of school. They had been runaways. And so, trying to take a kid that by their age may have been a ninth or tenth grade was really hard to mainstream. It became very obvious that we were going to do education on site. It became obvious that each kid, even though we were going to start with six kids, that they'd be on a different grade level so you're not going to be able to teach to six kids. You have to do one-on-one individual learning.

We partnered with a local charter school and we got the education piece set up before we ever had a kid and figured out what that was going to look like and hired a teacher, actually a former survivor as our first teacher to be able to understand the trauma that our kids have been through, to understand they develop mentally because of some of their trauma. There are delays and even in their learning and then also, that some of our kids were going to come in and didn't know how to read. So, they may 15, but they may be in first grade. The education piece is the first one we tackled from our program before we ever had a child, how are we going to do it and what are we going to do.

The other thing that we began to study and research was the issue of their trauma – complex trauma. And we began to search for who's even dealt with this kind of trauma locally, and that was really hard for us just to find mental health professionals who had seen or experienced or worked with kids that had this kind of trauma. It took a long time, and all of this we were doing in the beginning as we were trying to get a license in the state of California. That's a thousand-page document just to get a license. We had a team of five people that worked for a year just to get the license.

At the time, we didn't even know that California put a moratorium - there's no more group homes allowed in the state of California. And so, we were the last one that got grandfathered in, because we'd already started the process.

We basically figured out we needed a big piece of property, so that the girls could have certain amount of freedom, but we would have to be doing education and school at the house. And the whole time from the very, very beginning when I believed that it's a home, it's a home, I'm building a home. These are my kids. I wanted to create something that was home, that felt like a home especially when I began to realize a lot of these kids have never even had a home. And so, that means a refrigerator full of food, that means the ability to go out and play soccer in the yard or ride a horse or whatever that was, so I didn't want it to feel institutionalized at all.

This place is a home, and every girl that walks through the door, they got a welcome home party. I think all of them burst into tears when they walk through the threshold because it just feels like home. There are people there that already love you, and they're being prepped for that and tried to explain, but then it is a big place and it's mind-boggling. And it's more than most these kids have ever had, their own bed. A lot of the kids never even had their own bed.

It's important to me that the house was beautifully decorated. It was important to me that the rooms look like a teenage girl's room. They had their own space their own desk and that there's a big wide-open place where you'd snuggled up in blankets and hot chocolate and watch movies. And there's a place to go for hikes and go for walks down by the creek. So, in my mind, I was just doing what I've always done for my own kids was to make a home.

DT: Help me understand what happens at the home on a day to day basis.

Jenny: Absolutely. Courage House, I think what makes us different maybe than a lot of places is that the first place we start with is the girls' dreams. The very first conversation she has is, "What do you want to be when you grow up, what do you want to do?" And sadly, I didn't realize most of these kids don't even know how to dream. They've never even been given permission to dream. So for us, we want to expand their view of the world which many of our kids they have a one mile radius of a world sometimes that they've been in.

Even though we're doing therapy here, we're doing school here, we want to get them out into the world to do field trips. So I think every single day, they're leaving the property to go do something. There's a gym that gave all the girls a gym membership. So they've learned about physical fitness and their bodies and their health and nutrition, which they've never been taught. Many of them weren't even taught to brush their teeth, so that's a really important part. I often tell people I'm from Mississippi, so my dad always said if you exhaust your body during the day and your mind at school, then you sleep really good at night. These are the ways we address the high tendency of runaways is to exhaust their mind and their body every single day with new experiences.

As far as therapy goes, we are therapeutic from the moment they get up to the moment they go to bed. Every single thing they do has a therapeutic aspect to it. We have music therapy, we have equine therapy, we have art therapy, we have group therapy, we have individual therapy. I mean sitting at the table every night for dinner with a staff doing your "gratefuls" is therapy. It is our tradition every night to go around the table and say what you are grateful for.

And so, the entire environment, one mental health professional said to me, "What you created is like a cocoon, a perfect environment to accelerate healing." And so, when most mental health professionals, if you send your child and you go, you have an hour of time, but that mental health professional has no control over the environment you're in, so healing takes a long time. But when you've create this entire healing environment, the acceleration of that is huge. I'm not saying it's perfect, I'm not saying it's not messy, I'm not saying it's not hard, but…

DT: So, tell me about this perfect cocoon that you've created…

Jenny: [laughs] It's not perfect. That would be the wrong word. No, no. Just an environment that's conducive to healing. That's what we're trying to do. Now, you still take six highly traumatized teenage girls and put them all in a house together, and anybody who has a bunch of kids understands what that's like. It's the healing part - we're very, very intentional that every conversation even laughter is intentional. And we make sure there is laughter, and there's play every single day. So many of our kids have never played, they don't even know what it's like. The part that brings me more joy that anything is to just drive up and watch a water gunfight happening. It's intentional. Everything about it is pouring into them, healing and love and just value. I think that's the biggest thing when I said we start with their dreams. You can't dream if you don't believe you have value or worth.

And so, every girl that comes to Courage House sees me first. I don't know if we'll be able to do that one day when we have sixty girls, but right now, we've had 35 or 40 girls who have called Courage House home. They come up to our offices, and they meet me first. And I tell them the story I just told you. I tell them the dream that God put on my heart and that before I ever knew them that I've been fighting for them, that I've been praying for them, that they feel like my daughter, I've been looking for them, and that what was done to them is wrong and that there's a God in heaven that loves them, and there's this place. We're both crying by the end of it, and then she comes to Courage House's home.

I paint that picture for her so even before she goes, she has a sense of what she's walking into, and then I give her permission that at any day she doesn't experience that, she can come tell me, and I will make that right. And then, I promise her that our staff are loving and the best of the best, and the girls that are here want to be here and that she will go to sleep at night safe and that nobody's going to hurt her. And that every single day, somebody's going to tell her that she's special. Every single day somebody's going to say to her that you were created on purpose for a purpose and encourage her to be whatever she wants to be.

So, that's the part – the big part the vision for them. That's why they stay, that's why they go through the very difficult process of unearthing their memories, because they're going for their dreams.

DT: Tell me about Liz and how you came to meet her.

Jenny: We just finished the Believe In Me video. So, the song was written, tracks had been cut and production, and we just filmed up in Lake Tahoe and like everything these days, it gets posted on Facebook. I get an e-mail one day that said, "Thank you for what you're doing. I didn't know anybody knew, I am one of your girls."

And so, we exchanged e-mails a couple of times and even some phone calls. The first time we talked on the phone, she just called me "Mom" out of the clear blue skies and she said, "I hope that's not awkward." And I said, "Well, God always told me I was going to have daughters and so, I guess that's okay." Now, she is halfway across the country at this point in time.

She was still in a dangerous situation, and our phone calls and our e-mails would happen sporadically, but she always called me "Mom". And at the time in our history, we were doing the license as I described. We were trying to figure out education, we were trying to figure out mental health, but we had raised the money and bought this property so the house is empty.

We have an empty house, but we're opening a home for minors, and she was older than that. It wasn't quite clear what was going on except that this young woman had engaged me. I would tell her the dream, and I would tell her what we were doing and she became my adviser, if you will. "Well, you're going to need to do this, oh, my gosh, teenage girls, well, you better do this." So she became my expert if you will as we went through the process of opening Courage House.

Then, she called me one day, and she'd gotten out of the unsafe situation that she was in. She was being trafficked, and she was ready to move. I think she said, the very first thing I ever said to her is, "What's your plan?" because I am always about a plan, and she didn't have one at the time.

And she got herself out of that situation, she ended up moving out of the state to a homeless shelter, but she was moving closer to California than she was. And she lived and worked in a homeless shelter for a year and was in a dangerous situation and so just kind of stayed there. And as we built a relationship, it became clear, I just knew in my spirit that she's going to be at Courage House one day, and I thought she'd be on staff. I didn't know what, but I just knew she was going to be there.

Her time at the homeless shelter was coming to an end, and it was taking forever to get a license for minor children in state of California. So, it's kind of like a "duh" after a while, "We have an empty house, Liz needs a home and another daughter that I adopted." There's actually two young girls in my life that were homeless and over eighteen and needed a home. And so, we went to our board and we talked about it and our board was like, "Of course, why wouldn't we?"

We knew we weren't changing the vision about being home for minors because of that great need, but we thought, well, maybe this would be our first staff members, but we have an empty house. And so, we had a staff member that wanted to move in, and I asked Liz if she likes to come home and she said yes - so she boarded a plane. We never laid eyes on each other and on May 27th, I picked her up at the airport, and she called me "Mom", and she was my daughter. I don't know any other way to describe it.

And so, I brought her here to Courage House and she thought I was taking her into the boondocks. She was a city girl, and this place became her home. We didn't have therapist and programs and education, but Liz had put herself already through college. College was her escape, college was her place, reading and books. And so, even though she's been trafficked all these years, she managed to do that. Education became her passion for these kids. She knew education was an escape and a ticket out and she knew these kids were smart.

At the same time that we were developing a relationship and she was calling me "Mom", she was really passionate about the educational program and became the first teacher at Courage House for us and went back to school at William Jessup University and got her teaching credentials. She's about to get her master's degree, and so William Jessup has partnered with her in her education, so it's been amazing journey.

I'll often tell people, I didn't ask my husband if he wanted to adopt and I didn't mention it to my three sons. And so, Liz and my other daughter came for lunch one day and the first thing they said to my husband was "Dad" and he was like, "Oh, okay. What's that? All right." It's a little awkward for him, but he never had girls. And then, they came to dinner and then they spent the weekend and then they came for a week at Thanksgiving and they came two weeks at Christmas. And then, they just were our family. My boys call them their sister, and they are a family. Liz just changed her name legally to our name about a month or two ago, and she's the daughter, my other daughters, these are all my daughters, I don't know how to describe it.

But it wasn't part of the plan. When people say, "Was this part of the plan?" No, we just did what was in front of us one day at a time. And when Liz and my other daughter lived at Courage House, I'm always asked that question, you know, "Did the girls move in with you?" It was such a hard decision, when you have empty bedrooms, the emotional decision is a kid needs a home is to bring them in your home. But my husband works from home and I am doing this, and I have teenage boys in my house.

Courage House was the place that I was building for kids who had been highly traumatized, and I absolutely believe that every one of these kids needs a family just like Liz got a family. But there is a time, a critical time in their healing where they need 24/7 care, and I couldn't provide that where I was in life. That was so heart wrenching for me personally - like how can a mom not do this, but I also knew it was the right decision that there had to be this time of intense healing and people providing for that 24/7 before you can integrate kids into your home. And I'm just a firm believer that's why we build Courage House.

We believe we're going to prototype Courage House and build one in every city around the world that needs one.

I am so passionate about first giving these kids a time of stabilization before we move them into homes and families. Yes, they need a home and family. Yes, we want to do that if you have love in your heart. But I was totally, totally unprepared for the symptoms of their trauma. I've studied, I had read, I knew it in a textbook way, but I didn't know that I would be up all night for weeks on in sitting with a young woman who felt like she was a three-year old.

I missed holidays, I missed work, but I didn't know what else to do and so, that season with the older girls made me realize even more the importance of having a place where we can stabilize these kids emotionally. Then, the transition into a home and a family can be a good one, because the worst possible thing that can happen is to give a kid back, is to say you're too much, say I can't handle you here with the symptom.

That's why I'm super passionate about prototyping the building of Courage Houses around the world. We have 52 acres here, and we will have the ability after the permitting process to be able to build ten homes. We're really building a cul-de-sac, if you will. Think of a cul-de-sac, and it will be a home where six girls are in a home and then next door there'll be another home and all be connected and there'll be an activities. But we'll have our own school by then, be our own charter school and be able to do things on the site.

So, one cottage at a time. That's how we'll be able to bring more girls home. And in California that's important, because like I said, we can't open any new group homes, but we can build this property out for up to 60 maybe even 80 depending on the permitting process.

DT: Talk to the average person out there who is becoming aware of this issue. What do you want them to do? What is their response in the midst of this? What would you call them to?

Jenny: That is such a hard question. I know it should be simple, but it's hard and every single person asks me, "What can I do? Okay, you've messed me up, you've broken my heart. Either I want to kill somebody because they are hurting children or I'm paralyzed." And, I remember that paralyzed feeling. This is so big, and this is so evil. What can I do?

You don't need to do what I did. I know beyond a shadow of a doubt, I'm supposed to build homes. My husband and I have had our own business for 15 years. That's what I know how to do is to run a business and even though this is a home, to keep this sustainable to keep it open and keep it running, you have to know how to do that part. So, my easy answer for people is do what you love to do for these kids.

If you are a businessperson, help me figure out how to get sustainable funding for this where we can plan and we can build. If you're a musician, write a song for these kids. If you're an artist, paint a picture. If you're a filmmaker, make a film. But do what you love to do for these kids.

We've had a twelve-year old do a spaghetti dinner for us and raised $5,000. We've had artists, we've had compilation CDs now where they have given us the songs to be able to raise money and have sustainable funding. The dream all depends on being able to fund it.

But, you doing what you love to do, to me, that's the perfect marriage. Well, the first people I hired here was a rodeo queen. She'd been to Thailand and worked with victims in brothels, and she came to me and she's like, "I care about these kids and my passion is horses and you just married them for me." So, she teaches our girls how to ride horses. Combining your passion with this issue, that's how I believe that we'll take it off the table when the world becomes appalled.

I was raised in Mississippi, so I'm a product of the South and we grew up with the atrocity of slavery. It took a war in the South to end slavery, and it will take a war to end this kind of modern day slavery. But everything changed in the South when average everyday people became aware of the true conditions of the slaves.

I'm going to tell you about Courage House and the dream and the happy stories, but if you don't understand that we live in a world, in a country, in a city, where five and six and seven-year old children are being sold sometimes by their parents every single night for the pleasure and profit of another.

If you don't become enraged at that, then this issue will continue.

The day that the average person stands up and says "not in my world" and can imagine it happening to their kid, when that happens, this will go off the table and that is my dream. That is the mission and the vision of our organization is to end the trafficking of our children. I believe if you do what you know how to do and you're good at and you love and you put it towards this issue, then we can end this kind of slavery for our children.

Courage Worldwide
Sacramento, CA
www.courageworldwide.org

Courage Worldwide's vision is to engage 1,000,000 courageous people around the world to build 1000 homes in 100 countries in 10 years so hundreds of thousands of victims of sex trafficking can be rescued and restored.

LIZ

Sex Trafficking Survivor

Surrounded by cameras her entire life, Liz's earliest memories include being filmed for pornography and traveling the globe to be sold to men. She grew up attending a Catholic school and taking ballet lessons on a weekly basis, without any peers or adults ever asking what was going on behind the scenes. Education became her "escape" to deal with the trauma she was experiencing on a daily basis.

After seeing a video called *Believe in Me* on Facebook, Liz reached out to Jenny Williamson to say, "I'm one of your girls." Through emails and phone calls, Liz eventually broke away from the abuse and flew to Sacramento to start a new life with the type of family she always longed for.

DT: Help me understand - from the time you were a small child, what was life like for you?

Liz: From the time I was a small child, I grew up in a family that believed child pornography was okay and welcome and necessary in someone's life. So, I grew up with cameras and microphones around me, recording every move to where you would get so desensitized to it and when they introduced the abuse, you didn't care if there was a camera there. You were used to being watched. And because you were used to being watched, you were used to following rules and as long as you didn't – if you didn't break the rules, you'd be okay, but you always knew that they had the proof that you would break the rules.

And so, it was very abusive in that sense, because the minute they got inside your mind, they owned you. The minute that they could say "I heard what you said" or "I saw what you did" whether you actually did something or not, you felt trapped and so you stop fighting. It was actually really effective way to get a kid to feel controlled.

Some of my earliest memories as a child really aren't even memories, they are something hideous. And, I remember being locked in a bedroom where they said, "When you decide to follow our rules, we'll let you back out." Or, I remember not being able to eat or not being able to drink water, because they wanted to prove a point, and they wanted to prove a lesson that they controlled me, and I didn't control myself.

I remember wanting to go outside and play, and they would hold that as the big dangling carrot that as soon "as you do this for me, I'll do that for you." And I remember feeling so angry when they would lie, and you wouldn't be able to go outside and play, because they'd have another guy waiting.

I remember having to hide the books that I was reading from school underneath the beds, so they didn't see that I had something with me in that room that was good. I remember having a stuffed animal that I would have with me every night that I would try to hide from them, because I didn't want people who are so bad to ruin something else good for me.

I remember feeling lonely and wanting to feel normal because somewhere in my heart I knew that what was normal for me to be naked and lonely and hurting and so incredibly sad - that wasn't supposed to be the normal experience. That it wasn't supposed to be what you wake up with day in and day out. I remember wanting sheets on my bed and the only time you had sheets on your bed was when a guy would say he wanted this color and this style of sheet on the bed. I remember begging for pajamas, and I didn't have pajamas. And when they do that day after day and week after week, you forget to want something more because it's normal.

DT: You mentioned cameras and recording equipment being around you. How early do you remember this?

Liz: The first time I clearly remember being photographed and being filmed for pornography, I was five years old. I had a sense that it had happened sooner and earlier, because they would keep the cameras in the room. They would keep microphones in the room, so you stop feeling like that was odd You stop feeling like that wasn't out of place. Instead, you were a little girl on film all the time.

That camera owned your life and it owned your soul. Men would come in, and they would pay an obscene amount of money to do whatever they wanted to me on that camera and to take a piece of me home with them.

I remember thinking that they took my soul home with them, because I thought as a little girl that when you took a picture with a camera that you took your heart, too. It didn't make sense to me that they were taking pictures of actions. I literally thought that they would take my humanity with them, too.

I remember being told the only time I was allowed to look someone in the eye was if he had paid for it. Otherwise, you had to stare directly at the camera. You weren't allowed to look at people unless he was telling you what he needed you to do. So, I was a little girl who learned not to look people in the eye, and I was a little girl who learned not to speak unless you had permission. And those lessons stuck with me. While as I was growing up, I couldn't look people in the eye, and I couldn't talk easily because I was so afraid of what was going to happen if I broke that rule.

DT: Why do you think your parents were choosing to do this? What were the motives?

Liz: I truly believe that my parents sold me, because they were greedy and they're evil. I don't believe that it was for an economic reason. I don't believe it was out of desperation. I believe that they saw the profit that could be made in selling a child. Can I be honest and say you can call them purchasers instead of parents? You can call them a lot of things instead of parents.

DT: How would someone hear about you or be aware that they could purchase an experience with you at that age?

Liz: I think for a man to be able to able to purchase me, they came by word of mouth. Evil congregates together, and so one man would be able to see that another man would be interested in this. They would have a photo book of pictures that they had taken of me and the experiences that they could describe that I would able to offer. You know those instant Polaroid cameras? You know I learned to hate those things, because it was a cheap and easy way to be able to document something without having to keep it. For some men, they would learn about me through another friend or through a network. Then, they would write me letters to make sure that

I was real, and they would have me write them letters back because they really wanted to know that they were purchasing a young child.

They learned about me, and then they would tell their friends, and their friends would tell their friends. And then sometimes, there would be men who I would be out with - another adult - and they would just be able to tell. They would be able to know that they could ask to hurt me, and the adults around me would let them.

DT: As you began to get older, where you staying in one location or were you traveling? Help me understand that part of your life as you grew older.

Liz: As I grew older, I grew up in one house, but I did travel a great deal. For most of my 18 years, I had the same bedroom which I guess you could call stability in some sense, but it was an evil awful bedroom that had a lock on one side on the doorknob. I traveled a great deal. I would travel with a man. I would travel with him wherever he needed to go, because as long as you say that's your niece, who's going to ask questions? As long as the gentleman can say that's my daughter, who would ask questions? Because generally that relationship you can't really fake, and you wouldn't have asked questions. It doesn't look that odd.

I traveled in the U.S. I traveled the small towns and really big cities. I'd collect postcards and try to make it more normal. I traveled overseas. People would tell me how lucky I was to be able to travel, but what they didn't know was that if they had asked me if I liked it, if I enjoyed it, if I had a good trip, I would have looked them and said the truth that I was being bought and sold and that I don't exactly considered that a vacation.

DT: How many states and how many countries do you think do you traveled to over the course of 18 years?

Liz: 48 states and 22 countries. My passport is thick, and it's really difficult, because I wish when I was going through customs that they would look at a little girl and say - are you excited to visit whatever city this was. I couldn't have told you what city I was in. "Are you excited to see this town?" I can't speak the language, I have no idea where we are. "Do you know who you're meeting?" I wish they'd asked me simple questions, because the reality is I wasn't a liar. The reality is I have no loyalty to them except for the fact that I believed their lie that no one cared and no one would listen. So, I didn't speak up because if no one cares and no one is going to listen, what's the point?

DT: Who were the customers? Were these lower class, middle class, upper class? Were they known? Were they unknown?

Liz: The people, the men that would purchase time with me - they were men from all walks of life. There were lawyers who were well known, there were dentists and a doctor, and a priest, and a pastor. The men that abused me were congressmen. There were people of influence that told me they would use their influence to buy my silence, and I believed it. The higher up you go in sex trafficking, the more evil they become, the more wealthy they become, and the more grotesque.

There are people in this world that can hide behind a really attractive smile and sometimes as a little girl, you don't know whether their first name is actually what they say it is and so I just learned to call people "velvet sheets" or whatever I could pick out that would make sense to me. And then, sometimes they would tell you what name they would preferred to be called by. But the harder moments for me will be when they talked about their wife and their families. The harder moments for me would be when they talked about their daughter and how much they loved their daughter. That was hard.

I thought it was normal. I thought everyone did that to their daughter. I thought everyone made the little girl take off their clothes and to do whatever they said. I didn't know that wasn't supposed to happen. I had men who would write me letters and come to my ballet recitals. I thought it was normal.

DT: It sounds like you were going to school, you were taking ballet, you were going places...

Liz: Yeah. Like the library and the park.

DT: Did people not pick up on the fact that you're gone for periods of time to other countries? Did they not pick up on other signs?

Liz: I think a lot of people picked up on it, and I don't think they cared. It is inconvenient to care for a little girl that was being hurt. Yes, I went to ballet class; yes, I had bruises; yes, I had injuries that if you had asked me, I would give you the best excuse I could come up with. It wasn't true, but they didn't want the truth, they wanted something that was convenient for them.

And so, for most people I was a very clumsy little girl who have a lot of injuries like roller skating in the middle of winter, not true, but, okay, if that's how I got hurt. Or riding a bicycle to explain why your lower body hurt so much. I don't even know how to ride a bicycle, I didn't have bicycle. But most of the people that I was around were hurting me anyway, so they really didn't care. A man can still use your body even if it's hurting, and they'd probably prefer it because you're quieter.

Life was normal. Tuesday was ballet classes. I loved ballet class. Ballet class was the one time that it was actually okay to be quiet. You weren't supposed to talk at all. I excelled at that, so I'd have ballet class and for an hour and fifteen minutes, it was super, super normal, but then you would go into the changing room and you would get change and I know people saw bloody tights. I know that they saw bruises that weren't from falling off a bicycle or down the stairs. But I also don't think that they cared because as long as they didn't touch their daughter, who cares about me.

DT: Talk to me about school. From the time you were five to age 18, you were enrolled in public school, is that right?

Liz: Catholic school, not public school. Growing up I went to Catholic school from kindergarten until about tenth grade. So, when you grow up and you go to Catholic school and your family is very well known and very religious, when your family comes to check you out at school, they ask no questions because I am suddenly a very special little girl that gets to go on a trip somewhere. I am suddenly a very special little girl that should feel so loved that someone came and gave her a special lunch at school that truthfully had drugs in it.

School was my one favorite and my one safe place. School is the place where I can read books upon books and get lost in a different world for a little while. But school was also the place that I felt more trapped than ever because you're around normal people. You were around ordinary kids. You were around ordinary adults that actually don't come in your bedroom every night. And they think you're weird, when in reality you are lonely and you just wish somebody would ask why you're not eating that lunch that somebody brought you, because I would have told them that there were drugs in it and I didn't want it.

I wish somebody would ask me why I would fall asleep in class, it's because I was so tired at night time and it's actually a lot better if you're not sleeping when a John comes in the room. It makes it a little safer for your mind to at least be prepared for what you have to experience. A little less scary for a little girl.

DT: Help me understand why you were given drugs at lunch time.

Liz: There are a lot of different reasons you give a child drugs when they're involved in trafficking, when they're involved in being sold for sex. They could give you drugs that would make your cervix open up wider, so it didn't tear you. They'd give you drugs that could make you feel angry or scared or sad whatever emotion they were actually going for. If they give you the drugs early enough, it will settle in really well, because when you're filming pornography whatever experience that man wants whatever he needs, my face has to reflect, my eyes have to reflect, so it has to be genuine. So, if they genuinely want me scared, they'll give me something for that. And if they genuinely want me to be incredibly hyper and incredibly exuberant, they're going to give me something for that. And then if they need drugs where I don't need to remember anything at all and a guy just wants a body that's laying there that he can do whatever he wants, they'll give me that, too.

DT: At age 18, it sounds like there was a significant shift. What happened?

Liz: When I turned 18, one of the men that was so involved in selling me who I called my uncle - he passed away. And since he was the first one who had bought me at six and he was the first one who taught me how to be attractive and desirable to a man, when he died, I was so incredibly grateful for a few minutes I thought I could be free and I thought I could do something different. I thought that would meant that I wouldn't be sold anymore and I thought that it meant that another man wasn't going to own me. When my uncle passed away, I decided that I was going to go away and I was going to go to college because I knew that I was smart. I knew that I could read a lot of books. I figured that's mostly the only thing you had to do in college other than get in. So, I applied to colleges, and I knew or at least I thought I knew that if you can just get away from what you grow up in, you can do something different. I was afraid to be alone, but I was more scared to stay. I was afraid that what they said was true, that if I didn't have them, I wouldn't amount to anything, that I wasn't good in anything other than sex. I was afraid what they said was true, but I didn't want my body hurt anymore. So, yeah, the day that my uncle died, one of my favorite days of my life.

DT: And so, did you end up going to college? Did you run away? Did they help you go to school? What was your next step?

Liz: When I decided to go to college, I picked a college out of a guidebook, flipped open a magazine and said, "That is the college I'm going to go to." And I had enough money for a one way ticket, and I went down to college with about a suitcase and that was it because what did I need to bring with me? What did it matter? It didn't matter for anything. I went to college and I just wanted to be normal. I didn't know what normal was, but that's what I wanted.

DT: And, how did you leave? Did you run away because why would they let you go to college?

Liz: Right after my uncle passed away, they stopped locking the door, because they believed I wouldn't leave because I thought I was only good at sex. So, they stopped locking the door and then when I started to dream differently for myself, I didn't tell anyone, why would I tell someone?

I knew if you said it out loud, they were going to get in a way of that, they didn't want to lose their money. When my uncle passed away, he left me enough money to go to college for the first little bit, and I loved that I was 18 and that I could call a cab and go to the airport and pay my $89 in cash and go and have a different life because I had my passport. They weren't going to ask questions, because I had my ID. They weren't going to ask questions, because I was finally 18 and that mattered.

DT: What happened when you got there?

Liz: I went to college, and I really wanted to be a normal young lady except I didn't know how to be normal. I didn't know how to sleep normally or eat normally or be around people and have something to talk about other than sex. I know how to talk about that. So most of the time I was just really lonely because I didn't know how to let people in.

So for the first three months, I really enjoyed it. I enjoyed the classes except I would fall asleep in them. I enjoyed really normal experiences. Right up until when I decided that the college was closing for Christmas break, and where do you go when you don't have a family? Where do you go when you don't have a place to stay because the college is closing?

So, I went the airport fully intending to go back to the family that I grew up in, not because I wanted to and not because I love them, but because I didn't have another option. And instead, standing there waiting for a flight, this man starts to talk to me and right away having grown up around gross and evil men, I knew he was gross and evil, but that was super, super normal. And he tells me that I'm wonderful and that I'm beautiful. And he asked me what I'm doing and where I'm flying.

And I thought he was genuinely interested and so I tell him, "I don't really want to go back there, but it's Christmas and I can't stay at my college." And I believe he saw a need and he saw vulnerability, he told me that he loved me, and I believed it in the first 15 minutes because I wanted that desperately. I thought he was my way out and he was my freedom. He was what was going to mean that I didn't have to go back to the family I grew up in, so I moved in with him.

It only took him a week before I had told him everything about me, everything that I had always wished that somebody would know, every hurt and every fear and every bad memory, every weakness, and every strength I ever thought I had. I really wanted him to be my savior. I wanted him to love me and to protect me and to keep me safe at night.

And he wanted someone that knew how not to feel, who knew how not to act. He wanted someone that wouldn't ask questions when he said, wear this, do that, be with him. He wanted someone who didn't care how gross it was. He wanted someone who wouldn't complain and wouldn't talk back. And I was all of those things.

And I believe he love me. I believe that I was special. I believed him when he said that he would marry me one day. And I believed him when he said you have to be with these men, you have to take these pictures, you have to be in these videos because what was he doing my biological family hadn't, so he got me right there. He was not making me do anything I hadn't already done, so it made me feel trapped and invisible - feeling like this is all I am and this is all I'm ever going to be.

I am a girl that knows how to take her clothes off. I am a girl that knows how to sleep with men, and that's what I'm going to be. That's who I am, so I should get really used to the identity and that hurt because the dream inside me died, the hope inside me died. Anything that might have been good, didn't exist anymore. And the minute that hope doesn't exist inside me, he could do whatever he wanted.

I didn't dream about the future with him. I dreamed about what tomorrow was going to bring and the next day after that. I didn't think I'd live very long.

DT: How did you end up getting away from him? What was your next step?

Liz: Oh, my. There are a lot of stops and starts to get away from him. Every time I thought I would be confident enough to leave, every time I thought that I could do something different, I would talk myself out of it because it would be uncomfortable and it will be scary and I believe a lie that I couldn't do it. I believed that I wasn't worth it. Why would I fight for someone as stupid as me? Why would I put so much effort when I really don't matter when there's no value in me?

So, most of the time I talked myself out of it. But one morning I woke up and I started to feel angry at my heart. I was suddenly not in love with him as much as I used to be. Suddenly I was angry that he would be hurtful. And so, I decided that I needed to go back to school, and I needed to focus on something different. I needed to think that I could be good at something other than taking my clothes off.

So, I told him that I was going to go to school, I told him that it would make me better with every man that I would ever be with, because I would have something else to focus on. I would also have something else to focus on for me. I don't know whether he truly believed me or if he just thought it would pacify my and I would stop being grumpy.

So, I did school. I went to classes, and I showed up again with bruises, but more people would ask questions now. But I got really, really used to being able to say, "It doesn't matter. Nothing happened. Don't worry about it." But it wasn't as hidden as when I was just a kid. Suddenly, it's just out there. I can be promiscuous, I can be with an older man, he can show up at random times. I wanted to live a new life.

So, I went to college, and I loved my classes. I loved learning, but I didn't know how to make that final break. I always thought that he was going to be there, that if I went to school and I got my degree, eventually he would realize that wasn't the life I was supposed to have - that I was supposed to be home with him, and we were supposed to have a wonderful storybook and that selling me and using drugs and doing pornography wasn't going to be a part of it, so I wanted to prove it to him. But I loved school.

DT: My understanding is that you eventually saw a compelling video online that captured your attention. What was the video, and how did it impact you?

Liz: I saw a video of something that would completely change my life, and I didn't even know it. I was on Facebook, and someone that I didn't know had posted a video about this lady with a dream to build Courage Houses all around the world. And, there is this song on the video that said "believe in me".

I'm watching the video, and I don't know that it's about sex trafficking at first. I have no idea the story it's going to tell. I'm watching it, and I realized that it's my story. I'm watching it, and I realized that somebody cares, that it matters, that it's not supposed to happen, that you're not supposed to be sold. I'm watching it, and I realized that I want somebody to love me that much. I wanted somebody to build a house. I wanted somebody to have a dream for me. I wanted somebody to tell me I can do something different. But, the reality of my situation didn't seem to match up. So, I sent Jenny an e-mail and I said, "My name is Liz. This is my story. You told my story. This has been happening since I was six." And, she wrote back, and she believed in me and that I could do something different, and nobody had ever said that before. And at first, I didn't want to tell her that I was still with the bad guy.

She wanted to know what my plans were for the future. And I told her that I was in college, and I was graduating soon. But, I couldn't tell her that I didn't have any hopes and dreams.

My big dream was that I would die. My big dream was that this would stop, that I would stop being sold, because I didn't believe I could stop it for my-self. And Jenny wrote back and many, many e-mails and kept encouraging me and telling me that I could something different. And finally, one day I remember e-mailing her and telling her that the guy I was with had burned my arm on the stove. And, I remember her response wasn't what I thought it should have been.

She told me what he did was wrong, and there were so many exclamation points in that e-mail that I was surprised, because nobody had ever told me that they guys are wrong. I just wanted to explain to her what I did to make him do it. And, I knew in that e-mail that she really cared about me, and I wanted to make her proud. Suddenly, it mattered to me what someone else thought about my life. Somebody who didn't even know me.

I graduated from college, but instead of walking across the stage at my college, I went back to the guy I knew, because I didn't know where else I was supposed to go. I didn't know who I could call or what I could do. And for about two weeks, I just wanted to die - that was going to be my way out. Death was going to be the only way out of that, because I didn't know how to live. I didn't know how to be normal.

After about two weeks, I realized that video was still in my mind, those images were still in my mind and that I thought about Jenny's e-mails and I realized that she cared. I realized that she loved me. I realized that it would matter to her whether I live or whether I die, and I don't know that it had ever mattered to anyone before. And, that's what gave me hope to run. It gave me hope to do something different, because somebody had reached out and somebody said I see you, somebody said, you matter, you can do something different. Somebody could see a future for me and I could only see darkness, but I trusted that and I'm glad I did.

I ran away without shoes on. I ran away in the middle of the night. I didn't know where I was going, I didn't know what was going to be waiting for me, but I knew that I wanted to call Jenny. I knew that I wanted to tell her that I wanted a new life, too. I wanted it as much as she wanted it for me, because I had tried to die and that didn't work. I knew that I wanted to reach out to her because she treated me like I mattered. No one had ever done that before. I believed her in that e-mail that she said that she loved me.

DT: When you got off the plane in Sacramento, what did you see? What did you experience? What were those first moments like?

Liz: When I was on the plane to come to Sacramento, I thought, "Oh, my gosh! You're going to move somewhere, and they already love you, and they really care about you." I was so ready to get off that plane.

When I got off the plane, I remember looking at my phone and saw that I had a text message and it said, "Are you here?" And I was here. I wanted my bag to come through baggage so badly that I wanted to leave my luggage.

I was feeling nervous, and I was feeling excited and mostly just happy that someone was calling me family and that someone was calling me their daughter. That it meant forever, and I didn't know what forever meant. I didn't know what family meant, but I knew I never had it before not like this, not in a good way.

I wanted so desperately just to leave my luggage, and I walked outside and I saw my mom for the first time. And, I can't explain to you how your heart leaps to your throat because suddenly you're somebody's daughter, and it doesn't mean it's because of your body. You're somebody's daughter and it doesn't mean it's because of the price tag. You're somebody's daughter because they want you to be and because they chose you to be. You're somebody's daughter, and it means something good.

I hugged her for the first time, and I knew there is no turning back. I knew it didn't matter. It didn't matter how hard it was going to be, and it changed my life because nobody ever said that they wanted to do forever with me. Nobody had ever wanted to walk through life with me. It's probably the first time I was ever excited about the future. I couldn't have pictured it. I didn't know what it was going to look like.

DT: I know there were unique circumstances to you coming to live at Courage House, but what are some of the things you experienced here on the property that begin to bring hope and healing and transformation to you?

Liz: The first moment I walked into Courage House and I had a bed with sheets, it was incredible. I jumped up and down on the bed, because it was mine, because it meant that there wasn't going to be anybody sneaking into my bed in the middle of the night. It was so much freedom, it was terrifying.

I remember the first time I was able to lock a bathroom door and truly know that it would stay locked, because I wanted it be locked in my house. I remember the first time I walked outside in the dark, and I felt safe. I remember walking around in the Courage House property and testing out talking, practicing how to talk, and how to have conversations with people. I would talk to the dogs. I would practice being a new person.

When I moved here, I didn't know what my favorite color was. I didn't know what my hopes and dreams were. I didn't know how to be me without feeling like I wanted to come out of my skin. Courage House was my safe place. I would go, and I would sit in the garden for hours not because I garden, but because it was mine and because it was safe. I would sit and I would journal, and I would suddenly dream about a future that I never thought I would have.

DT: Tell me attending William Jessup University - the experience of going back and getting your teaching credential. What did that mean to you?

Liz: Going to Jessup and getting my teaching credential was the craziest decision I made in my new life. I believed I could have a future and I believed that I mattered. It was that first giant step forward. Going to Jessup, I wanted to be a teacher, because I knew what it felt like to be invisible, and I didn't want any kid to ever feel invisible if I could be their teacher. I wanted to be the teacher that can make kids feel seen and special and valued and loved.

Going to Jessup was one of the first places I made friends. It was one of the first places that I had to stretch and grow and become a new person. Jessup meant more to me than just classes. Jessup was the place where I had to practice my new identity and start to own it and believe that I had potential, believe that I had a future.

Jessup was the first place that somebody told me I was cute, and I stared at this young man, and I said nothing back because I didn't know what you're supposed to say. I literally had no idea what to say, so I just looked back at my book, and I continued reading. Later, I told my parents what happened, because I thought it was weird - I mean really weird.

And they said, "What did you say back?"
I said, "I didn't say anything back, I just kept reading my book."

I later had to go and apologize to this young man, because it's not very polite not to say thank you when someone tells you that you look pretty. Jessup was a growing experience. That was a funny time.

DT: People encounter you now would have no clue what you've been through. If they found out, they would probably think to themselves, "Everything's turned out so great for her, everything has come together." What is life like now? Are there challenging times? Are there good times? Or, is it a completely new life?

Liz: My life is more wonderful than I ever could have pictured it, but it's also been harder. How do you start a brand new life with brand new people and you believe in your future suddenly, but you also remember your past? How do you move forward and be a new person? That's been a tough question. But it's been wonderful and safe even when you don't sleep at night and you have so much anxiety and you can't breathe, but you have people around you who say, "Okay, I love you. I'll pray for you. Breathe, that would be helpful." Because when you forget to breathe, they tell you to breathe.

It's been difficult. It's hard to learn how to make friendships and how to keep friendships. It's hard to forget what you've known. It's hard to move forward when you believe in the invisible rules in your head that you're breaking every day, that you're talking and you don't ask for permission and you're looking people in the eye and you don't ask for permission. Until one day, that becomes normal and that becomes ordinary.

I can't tell you that exact moment, but suddenly one day I liked who I was. Suddenly one day I knew that I had value. Suddenly one day, it really didn't matter to me what had happened in the past not because it wasn't ugly and not because it wasn't awful or because it's not my reality now. I remember it every day, but I don't have to live that way. So now, yeah, most people can't tell. There is no marker on my forehead that says trafficked - that says sold. I think they think I'm goofy. I think they think I'm loud and that's okay, but I love to be able to tell people my story when it's right and when it's appropriate and when they will hear it and respect it for what it's worth.

I love my life now, and I'm grateful for what happened to me, because I love using it for good. I love the moment that I can look into another girl's eyes and say that I understand what it means to be sold, and then I can promise her that I understand what it means to be free, and I can promise her that she can feel that way, too. Healing has been hard, healing has been tough, healing has made me want to quit on most days. But, why would you quit when you have a family? Why would you quit when you have everything you ever dreamed of? As long as the past stays in the past, I don't care.

DEENA GRAVES

Founder of Traffick911
Dallas, TX

An information meeting at her church caused Deena Graves to start asking the question, "How could this possibly be happening in our country?" Through hours of research, she learned that we have a segment of society - "throwaway kids" - who have little value to their parents or their communities.

With a three-prong vision of prevention, rescue, and restoration, Deena founded Traffick911 and eventually opened their first aftercare home called Triumph House. Situated on 168 acres outside of Dallas, the home is a refuge for minor victims of sex trafficking as they find hope and healing from their trauma.

DT: When did you become aware of sex trafficking?

Deena: About four years ago, I was working at Texas Instruments on one of the leadership teams for a business unit there, and it was right when the economy crashed and we were laying off almost half of our work group. My church had a speaker coming in to talk about sex trafficking in a third world country, and I was so exhausted. It's like - I want to support this, but I can't because, you know, this is women and prostitution halfway around the world. And in my mind, I live in my own little civilized bubble, I can't imagine this happening anywhere in the world, didn't have a clue what human trafficking was.

But, I ended up there and during the course of it, she showed photos and a video of children they had rescued from sex trafficking. And, it just totally rocked my world. I couldn't believe this could happen anywhere. And one of my friends is a Dallas police officer, and he had just been part of a huge FBI initiative called Innocence Lost where they rescue kids from across our country.

I made a comment, "Philip, well, I can't believe this happens in third world countries."

And Philip said, "Deena, this happens here."

And I said, "No way. We are a civilized Christian country, we will not do this to our children."

I just started doing hours and hours of research, and that's when I realized we actually do it to our children. The only difference is we're really good at covering it up. Third world countries - it's out on the street where you can see it, but in our country, we hide it.

DT: After hearing about the issue, what was your next step? How did you respond?

Deena: I just did research for a few months and found out that this is a huge, huge epidemic in our country happening to our American children. We have something in our country called "throwaway kids", and they have no value in our society. Juvenile detention tells us that they will have a run-away brought in by law enforcement, and they'll call parents, and parents won't even call them back. These kids have zero value.

And so, the more research I did, the more I found out that not only are they just thrown away by their families and lured into the webs of the traffickers because of that, but then the system fails these children as well, and we don't have any resources for them. And so, the more I dug, the more I realized that there's not much being done to help these kids.

I ended up quitting my job and it was definitely a battle with God. I was like - this is the first time in eternity You've made a mistake. I don't know anything about non-profits. I don't know anything about this issue, but He wants me and I ended up quitting my job and starting Traffick911 about four years ago now, and it's been just an incredible journey.

DT: Talk to me about Dallas and why Dallas is unique in regards to sex trafficking.

Deena: Okay. So, Dallas, according to the FBI, is in the top thirteen for this crime. And if you think about it, our central location in the middle of the country, you know we can be anywhere on the mainland within three or four hours. So it's easy to use the Dallas Fort Worth area North Texas as a hub. You can stay there, then move your girls out to other areas to be able to sell them.

We also have major highway systems, a lot of trucks stops, Greyhound bus stations, many factors that make this a prime recruiting ground and a prime selling ground as well.

DT: Tell me about the role of gangs in this issue.

Deena: Anywhere you have organized crime or gangs or the mafia – the Mexican mafia - you have our American children being forced into sexual slavery. This is so profitable, and there is such a small chance of being caught, and they've got a reusable commodity. The gangs are actually laying aside their feuds, and they are working together to sell our American children.

We have one little girl who is in our safe house now - she was traded by her mom at 13 to an organized trafficking ring in exchange for a pickup truck. And for two years, she was just brutalized by this group of people who were using her for their own profit and pleasure. Many times what they will do is they will force these kids into other crimes as well, so they will make them run drugs, they'll make them attack people, all kinds of other things.

One of the huge things that we do is we go into juvenile detention - also the prison system - and we find these children hidden under other charges in there. We're just trying to bring to light that these children are not criminals, they're victims who are being forced into horrific things so that other people can make a profit of off them.

DT: How did you start Traffick911 and eventually the aftercare home, which is called Triumph House?

Deena: We started with just a dream to have our American children have value again and to be able to give them hope. And so, we actually started with nothing. It was just a handful of people that I knew who came together at the table and said, "What can we do about this?"

We developed a three-prong strategy of prevention, rescue, and restoration. And one of the biggest things in my research that I found was that our American children are going to jail while the people who are doing this to them are pretty much walking away free and clear or else with just a slap on the wrist.

One of the very beginning pieces of our strategy was to go into juvenile detention and try to find these children. And, that's how we got started and through that we began building relationships with juvenile justice, CPS, law enforcement, and really partnering with them to take our American children back - get them out of the jail cells and out of the arms of these predators.

DT: Talk to me about that program. How many juvenile detention centers do you go into?

Deena: One of our closest partners is the juvenile justice system in Texas. We currently go into five county juvenile detention systems and take our "Traps of a Trafficker" program for the girls in there. We also are expanding into three other counties right now.

The curriculum lays out the facts for them of how these people trick, trap, and lure them into their web. And, we take that into schools and youth groups and boys and girls clubs and all kinds of places. Before we go into juvenile detention, these children are living it and so, they are frightened to tell their story to authorities because of what the pimps have brainwashed them to believe and because the systems in many cases have failed these children.

And so, when we go in and we do the Traps, which is very real with them, and we present it in a way that it's on their level and so, when we do, they just pour their story out to us. And then, when they pour their story out, we were able to use that to get them help and then to get the bad guys off the street as well.

DT: Why would you go into juvenile detention centers to do this presentation? Like why there versus public high school or private high school?

Deena: Well, we do public high school and in middle schools and any place where there are kids, we take this program. But, the reality in our country is these children are going to jail for the crime committed against them. And, just like I said earlier in our conversation, they are hidden under other charges because these people make them do other things during the course of their captivity.

We go in, and we take this program in, so that they can share their story and get the help that they need. Our children shouldn't be sitting in jail for what other people have done to them.

DT: When did Triumph House open, and what do you offer?

Deena: Triumph House is our safe home for these children that we are identifying inside of juvenile detention and that come to us by other means. We opened in December of 2013. On the property, we have an existing 7,000 sq. ft. house that was renovated, and in this house, we can take up to six girls.

All of these children are begging us, "Please do not put me in another group home." They have spent their entire life, their entire childhoods in and out of juvenile detention and group homes, drug rehabs, psych hospitals and the way that these people lure them into their web is by offering them protection. It's the law of survival, and they're desperate for family.

One little girl said, "I would rather have sex with a stranger every day, than sex with my daddy every day."

What we're working to do in Triumph House is creating that family unit that they've never had. So none of our homes will have more than six girls in it. The original 7,000 sq. ft. home, we are slowly ramping up because we are taking the worse of worst cases, the little girls who have been tortured. Their healing is very lengthy and the amount of torture that they've lived through are things that you cannot even begin to wrap your mind around.

So, the 168-acre ranch starting with the original 7,000 sq. ft. house on the property. We have an architect who's done a site development plan for us, and we will be building other homes on the property. Again, no home will have more than six girls, every house either will have house parent or house parents or a house mom.

The first house has a house mom in it, and we also have shift staffs, so day staff, awake night staff. They monitor our camera systems if the girls have nightmares or any of those kind of things. We have a complete holistic program to wrap around these girls. So on-site schools, our trauma counselors come onsite to work with the girls. We have creative therapy, huge believers in creative therapy. So many things that these kids can heal from outside of the counseling room that they can't in.

So, for example we have an 8,000 sq. ft. barn doing equine therapy. We have other animals on the property, art therapy is a huge part of our program. So just many different things to help them completely heal and get to that point where they can live a triumphant life.

DT: Take me through an average day. Help me understand what they do.

Deena: These children are desperate for boundaries and structure in their life. Again, 80% of the victims of this crime came from very dysfunctional families where they're being abused in their own home, and they've never had structured, they've never had boundaries. So, our program is extremely structured. They get up in the morning, they have breakfast, get dressed.

We have our girls get dressed and not just hang out in their pajamas in the home, because we want them to understand in life there are certain things you have to do to be successful. They get up, they get dressed, they go to school. After school, they either do their counseling or they all do other various structured programs - maybe some kind of group counseling. The horses are part of their program, the arts, whatever it is for that particular day.

And, we want to teach them that they have a voice. And so, for example, we were doing school five days a week, Monday through Friday, and then they had to their chores on Saturday. Well, the girls wanted to be able to sleep in on Saturday, so once a week, we have a house meeting and they put together a plan. They came to the house meeting and said, "Can we do school longer four days a week, do our chores on Friday and get to sleep in on Saturday and then have more fun time?" And so, we listen to that voice. They have a solid plan and so that's our new structure now based on the girls' input.

DT: That's great. Talk to me about success that you're seeing.

Deena: We met one of our girls in the prison system - prison for children - and in there for charges that this trafficking ring had made her do. And so, we worked with the state and with the judge and she came to Triumph House.

She told us that during the time she was being held in captivity and during the time that she was in the prison system, she was just begging God, "Please send me someone. Send me someone to help me get out of this."

We've only been open two months, but we are already seeing so much hope return to her, we're seeing the glint return to her eyes, and she writes me notes all the time. She drew me a drawing. She's a great artist, and she drew me a drawing and she – she just said, "You know, I clung and I believed and in the midst of the hurricane God sent me a rainbow."

So, just getting to see their hope coming back to them. One of the people in the prison system worked very closely with us to get her there, because this is a new paradigm for the system - to let the kids to come to a place like this. She actually drew a charcoal of Jesus and on it she wrote his name and said, "Thank you for believing in me and having hope and giving me hope again." So, just seeing – seeing that hope come back to them is incredible.

She spent several months in prison after being held in captivity for a couple of years by this group, not too long after she came to us, she wrote me this note and she said, "When you came to talk to me at TYC, you made me realize that God has amazing plans for me and that after hurricane comes a rainbow. I never thought I could be in a place where I can get healed. This place is the best experience ever. I'm glad God put you in my path because it inspires me a lot and gives me hope for a new life and a better life."

And then she goes on at one point of saying, "One day I'm going to work for Traffick911 and help other children as well."

We are seeing great success out of this, but the tragedy is that we have found more than 80 little girls sitting in juvenile detention or prison who are victims of this crime, and they are desperate for place for healing. We're having to turn them away every single day as well as other safe houses in the country are having to do the same thing.

One of the greatest ways that people can engage in this is by helping us build our safe houses, so that we can take more of these children, get them out of the jail cells and out of the arms of the people who are buying and selling them for their own profit and pleasure.

DT: What is your vision for this 168 acres?

Deena: We are working to build it out. Right now, we have a site development plan that our architect has done for us. We've got the 8,000 sq. ft. state of the art barn, and across from it will be a life center that will house our on-site school, our counseling, offices, that kind of thing. And then on each end, we will build out houses that will each hold no more than six girls. In the middle of that will be sports court.

You know these little girls have had their little bodies completely destroyed, and they need physical healing as well as the psychological and educational. So, we have a lot of things built into our site development plan for the physical healing; the sports courts, swimming pool.

We're in the process right now of building a ropes course with this crazy structure we have on the property that we're not even sure what it was intended for. We're going to build a nature trail. We have three ponds on the property where they'll be able to follow the nature trail and then go out and just sit and journal.

There's a lot of healing in journaling or drawing. Our girls are very creative, and they get a lot of healing through either drawing or writing. One of our girls likes to write rap songs, so, you know, whatever it is that brings them healing, we want to be able to support that on the property.

DT: It's amazing all that you've been able to accomplish in such a short period of time. Why are you leveraging your life in this way?

Deena: It's like I told you in the beginning - in our country, we somehow have gotten to the point where it's okay with us that we have throwaway children.

Right now in the state of Texas alone, according to the National Center for Missing and Exploited Children, there are 47,000 open missing children files. Where are all these children?

One of our little girls was on the streets of Dallas being bought and sold for an entire year while her photo is in the National Center for Missing and Exploited Children's database just a few miles – 20, 30 miles from her home, and no one knew what was happening to that child. Our children don't have a voice. They're silently begging us to help them. And so, I just can't sit by and let our children be totally ravaged by people who just want them for profit and for pleasure.

There was a research study done by a university asking men why they pay for sex, and the overwhelming majority of the answers were all about power and control.

According to the FBI, our children who are living this life have average life expectancy of just seven years.

They're dying from murder and suicide and disease and drugs and we can't just sit by. We don't have time to wait. They're dying underneath our noses.

DT: If you were to speak to the average person who's just hearing about this, how can they help?

Deena: We always tell people who want to volunteer for Traffick911 is - figure out where you're passionate and where you're gifted. Those are the two key areas.

For example, we have a psychiatrist that sees our girls pro bono. We have an architect who's helping us develop the site plans. We have a doctor that we can call and get medical advice from. She's done all of our medical policies and procedures. We have artist who comes out and helps the girls. We have someone do musical lessons with them. Whatever your gifting is, whatever your talent and your passion, there's a place for it for these children who are living this.

DT: Last question. What is your dream or hope for America five, ten years from now in regards to this issue?

Deena: The biggest challenge that we have is getting people to believe this happens in our country. These children are not seen as credible. No one believes them, and all the funding goes to other countries. Our hope is that children in our country will have the same value as people in other countries. It is much easier to send your money to a third world country instead of getting your hands dirty right here.

Again, we have this whole segment of children in our country that we call throwaways. We want to eradicate that term, and we want to make every child in our country have value and human dignity.

Traffick911
Dallas, TX
www.traffick911.com

Traffick911 is a team of passionate people driven to stop the sale of American children into sexual slavery for the profit and pleasure of their perpetrators.

STACIA FREEMAN

U.S. Director of Hope for Justice
Nashville, TN

Initially motivated by emotion, Stacia soon realized that her background in the medical field uniquely equipped her to make a significant contribution in the fight to end sex trafficking. As the U.S. Director of Hope for Justice, she has the opportunity to lead their staff as they train first responders and professionals, promote quality restoration, and create a network of service providers - all while working alongside their expanding international team.

Stacia is leading the charge as Hope for Justice seeks to found a model aftercare home in Nashville as a place of restoration for minor victims of sex trafficking as well as a training center for other aftercare homes around the nation.

DT: How did you become aware of sex trafficking? Was this something that was new for you?

Stacia: It was new for me. I had not never ever heard of child sex slavery or trafficking. When I heard about it and I researched it, I couldn't believe, first of all, that I've been living in this country and had never heard about the issue. It wasn't even an issue of being a mother, that made me want to get involved, but it was the issue of just being a fellow human being that I felt like I couldn't know about something so dark and not be willing to engage in whatever I could do to make a difference.

DT: When you first heard about the issue, were you thinking people were making this up? Did you think it was outlandish? What were you thinking?

Stacia: I think it was really hard for me to bridge the gap between what was slavery and what was prostitution and understand how they were related - to understand that nobody really sits down when they're growing up and says when I grow up I want to be a prostitute. I had to break down some of the barriers of some of the mindsets that we form around that issue.

I think that I thought of the little children on the commercials that you see in the middle of the night when you stay up late and, you know, it's really sad and it's asking you to dig in your pocket and send money. I was thinking this is just an issue that happens overseas. It's not happening here in the United States. It's something that happens in faraway places, and we can send money there and we can be engaged as much as we can be, but it's not something that's happening to America's children, because that wouldn't happen here.

I just thought we were too civilized to allow something like that to go on, and I thought really and truly there were too many people that would be concerned about that issue to ever allow that to happen. What I found is most people didn't know about it, and then when we found out, there was this desire to justify the behavior and to justify why that was occurring. "Well, her mother was this or her father was this and therefore, she became this and that was just a natural progression of where she came from."

It was a journey for me to start to understand what happens in someone's life that causes things to go so wrong. We know that no one desires to be used and held against their will and forced to do the unthinkable, the unspeakable over and over and over.

DT: How did you get involved with Hope for Justice?

Stacia: I'm a clinician by training and had worked in the medical field in research development with a product company that works with newborns and newborn health. I had stopped to have children and really had no experience with non-profits. I didn't know a lot about this issue and when I found out about it, I was just a willing participant in terms of what can I do, how can I make a difference, and it just kind of evolved from that point.

I wouldn't say that I went willingly. I think I was constantly saying, "Yeah, I'm really not equipped to do this, I'm really not experienced enough. I don't know anything about this. I don't think that I have any tools or skills to benefit." But, then I found out that I actually did, that there were things that I had done before that were beneficial to this field.

DT: Over the last seven years, how have you grown as an individual and a leader?

Stacia: As a leader, I have learned about myself and my abilities and obviously my shortcomings. The best leaders are people who recognize the areas they are not as strong in and surround themselves with people who really fill in the gaps. I've been really fortunate that the kind of people who come along side me have been people who are really great in the areas that I'm really not good at. I think that this issue is so big that it takes a team. It really takes a team approach if we're going to make a dent in the issue at all, it's going to take an army of people to address it.

I'm still growing and learning, I'm still evolving. Whenever I feel like know it all, then it will be time to move on, because I feel like in any area that you always want to be in a situation where you're continuing to learn. The field is changing, and we're learning a lot from the international people that have been serving trafficked youth for 25, 30, 35 years and there's a lot to gain from them as well. We're learning from people who have served youth in other areas and exploitation in other areas - from adult populations and those things are valuable as well.

I just feel like my past experiences have enabled me to bring something of value to the table, but I have never stopped seeing it as a partnership.

DT: Tell me what Hope for Justice is all about.

Stacia: Hope for Justice is about quality. It's about empowering people to do things well. I think one of the biggest frustrations to me coming into this area was that so many people were just trying to meet a need, and they were doing it for noble reasons and maybe to the best of their ability, but it wasn't the best. I worked in healthcare, and I saw the responsibility of hospitals, surgical centers, newborn nurseries, and the standards that they were really held to, and it bothered me that in this field we didn't have any of that.

And so, Hope for Justice started to address standards of care and creating a community of people who were willing to get engaged in the process by providing not just care, but the *best* care so that individuals who were being served through the program could develop skills that really help them achieve success.

In order to do that, we had to define success, and the thing I think that's tricky in working with this population is success is different for different people. So, some person may be able to achieve one thing that another individual will not be able to achieve. Programming and measurements for success must be individualized.

Something I think is really valuable to the process is the restoration piece and not only just providing a bed or a place to stay, but providing quality programming so that people who have been exploited can get back on their feet and can impact their communities in ways that matter. They don't have to be prisoners of where they came from, but they get to look forward to the things to come.

I think Hope for Justice went from being an organization that focused on the travesty of the bondage moving towards looking at the hope of the future. I would say that we really are an organization that wants to focus on the future and the hope of the future and not the darkness of the past.

DT: Tell me about the Hope for Justice Professional Providers Network. What does it mean to be a part of the network?

Stacia: The Professional Providers Network is an association made up of organizations that address the issue of sex trafficking and exploitation around the world, but primarily in the United States.

It creates a network where you can cross-refer clients in different areas that might need placement, and it also creates community so that you can share experiences. It gives us the opportunity to research and provide data so that we can further understand what creates quality in that setting.

It started because we had a victim we were helping find placement, and in doing that, we couldn't find any services for her at all. No one was equipped to handle the level of mental health needs she had. I had some email addresses of people who were starting to address the issue domestically, and I called them all together and asked, "Would you be willing to sit down with us and talk to us about what you're doing? What are your biggest challenges, and how we might can come alongside you and help you with that?"

In that meeting, there was a doctor from Ohio, Dr. Jeff Barrows, who's really involved in writing a lot of opinion pieces on health consequences of trafficking and what the state of the issue is in the United States. And, he was starting a home in Ohio, and we started talking about professional networks. Because he was in the medical field, he had been part of a professional association and because I was in healthcare, I had been part of a professional association, and we just kind of dreamed about it together.

We believe that there's strength in numbers and so it really allows us all to come together and share our experiences and expertise. "Hey, we had that situation, and this is what worked for us." It also creates a network. So, if there's a home that's full and can't take someone in, there are 25 other homes that function along the same premise. You can call and say, "Do you have availability to take a case from Texas?" Sometimes, for safety reasons, victims need to be placed in other areas, so it does a couple of things.

It addresses the quality care, it creates a network to place victims, it creates community, a professionalism, and we do a lot of research to look at testing different like counseling models and looking at the layout of homes and the staffing requirements and staff ratios and things like that. How do you achieve a level of success that can be repeated by other people that want to provide the service?

DT: Obviously, there's a lot of darkness surrounding this issue. Give me some hope. What comes to mind we you start looking for hope?

Stacia: I think one of the hopeful things is the willingness of organizations to partner. In Nashville, for instance, we have six to eight different organizations that are meeting different needs. There is a juvenile outreach program that's starting to develop - doing outreach in the juvenile facility. There's Magdalene House and Thistle Farms that create jobs and placement for adult women who are aging out of prostitution - many of them who were victims of trafficking. And then, Hope for Justice who does a lot of training and outreach, and we are headquartered here. The most successful communities are the ones that address it from a continuum of care perspective, understanding that it takes many pieces to address the issue. I see a lot of hope in that, when people don't need to have ownership of everything.

I also see hope in the fact that people aren't focused on where we are, they're focused on where we're going. And I think that is very hopeful, because when you look at a little girl and she thinks that what you want to hear is what she did yesterday before she was picked up or before she had the opportunity for a future, and you teach her it's not about what you did yesterday, it's about what you have the potential to do tomorrow. Then, she starts telling you about what she really wants to be when she grows up and where she wants to go to school and what she wants to study, and she starts engaging in conversations about the future and not just wanting to talk about the past. When you start to see people kind of come out of that, that's really hopeful.

For me, the reason that I do this is because if you have the opportunity to help one person stop defining themselves by their past and look forward to the future, then it's a rewarding way to serve. That's pretty incredible to get to be a part of that on some level. We recently had someone reach out to us via Facebook, and she wasn't asking for help. She was just simply saying, "Wow. I love what your organization does. I wish you'd been around twenty years ago when I really needed help and, you know, I pulled myself up from the bootstraps and I kept going."

She's quite remarkable because of what she's been able to achieve and accomplish with really no help at all. She and I talked for a while, and we ended up helping her find a therapist, and she's been going to therapy. She's been communicating, "This is amazing. I didn't even know that I needed this."

That's so great, when you can just provide services for someone just by giving them options so that they don't feel like, okay, I'm kind of in this alone, but I'm doing it, you know, I'm trudging ahead, it's all good. They don't even realize the things that they still need to do, and it's great to get to be part of that. I see that as very, very hopeful.

Sometimes, when you focus on the numbers and the sheer magnitude of the problem, it can be paralyzing. You just sit there, and you just want to write a check and be done with it. But, when you focus on that one little girl or that one little boy - who they used to be, but now they're this, now they're in school, now they've graduated, now they are moms and dads and leaders in their community - that's really hopeful. I think that's what we should really all be striving for.

I always say that the goal in this is to work ourselves out of a job, and we hope that the issue will be addressed to the level that we won't be doing this anymore. Then, we'll move on to the next thing that matters. So, I think that is all part of the hope.

DT: How many aftercare homes are there in the United States at this point?

Stacia: It's estimated that there are around 40 homes in the US dedicated to specifically serving the needs of sex trafficking survivors both adults and minors. The numbers are constantly changing and there may be facilities that have bed space for this population but not specialized programming. The most conservative estimates for need say we have roughly 100,000 US children exploited in the sex trade each year, so that indicates that there is still a need for qualified programs.

DT: Specifically here in Nashville, why is Hope for Justice focused on opening an aftercare home for minors?

Stacia: The main reason that we are dedicated to opening a home in the Nashville community is because we're housed here. We're part of the tapestry of this community, and we want to be an organization that practices what we preach. We've been saying for a long time - this is the way that you build quality housing for victims - so we want to take those resources that we've developed over the past five years and really put them into practice.

One of the biggest shortcomings that we see in organizations is they approach everything from an emotional standpoint. "I know the need, I really want to get involved in the issue", but they don't do their homework beforehand.

Because we completed a feasibility study to address the needs in Nashville, we started to understand the make up of the community in terms of who the stakeholders are and the other professionals and organization that are serving the population in some capacity. We saw that we bring value to the table based on our experiences and our areas of expertise. So often, what happens is people just address one piece of the problem, and unless you look at the issue from a consistency perspective, then you're likelihood for success decreases.

Because Nashville has such a great community of people willing to engage and work together, it really provides us with the consistency that victims need - from the minute they are identified until they transition out of long term care - and then even beyond that as you look at educational opportunities and employment opportunities in the community.

DT: Where are you in the process of developing this home? Give me a big picture of the current state of your planning.

Stacia: Well, you always want everything now. I think I've learned in the process that sometimes there's a gift in the waiting because you learn a lot during that process. We've met with key stakeholders in the area and obviously some donors in our community that are very committed to seeing this home open. Right now, the program piece is in place and ready to go. It's mainly looking for the physical facility and then raising the operating budget for the first two years. We need to raise about $5 million in order to make all of that happen. We are looking for the right piece of property and the right location that really allows us the growth that's necessary to expand - that allows us to do teaching and training. In reality these projects can take several years to come to fruition. So, in the interim, we are addressing the need in phases beginning with outreach and education as well as out-patient services for at-risk youth

If we don't link arms and engage and start sharing what I know and what you know and start really sharing information, I don't know that we'll ever really address this issue in our lifetime. And if our goal is really long-term to eradicate sex trafficking, it's going to require partnership. So, the model home in Tennessee really opens the door for that partnership by allowing our experiences to impact others, and that's really the dream.

DT: How can people get involved in this effort? How can someone take action if they're not a professional?

Stacia: I think you we have to be honest that emotionalism drives the process for a lot of us. I mean, it's the reason that I got involved. I didn't know that any of my past experiences would equip me for any of these. So, I think that all of us come to this going, okay, now that I'm aware of the issue, the first step is just being willing to engage because a lot of people kind of plug up their ears and close their eyes and go, enough, don't tell me anymore. So, just being willing to engage is really the first step, but then where do you go from that?

Being willing to build a team of people that are strong in areas where you're not strong, makes a more viable project long-term. So, I always say pick your passionate, and then decide to how much you're willing to be engaged. Are you a speaker? Can you go and talk about the issue and get other people educated and involved? Are you more passionate about the demand side? Are you more passionate about the restoration side? Are you more passionate about the prevention side?

Domestically, we are really starting to see a great opportunity for churches and average citizens to get involved by serving the at-risk areas.

Does that mean you show up and have lunch with the kid that maybe doesn't have anyone who is a role model in their life? Or, you can go read at a school in an at-risk area. Maybe you can train teachers to recognize signs of exploitation so that they can make referrals. If we don't address the root causes of the problem - poverty, violence, neglect, unstable families - and start to reach out in those areas, we'll always be addressing it after the fact. There is more than enough work for everyone to contribute to solutions.

I think it's just being willing to think outside the box and not thinking that, "Oh, that this means I can only be engaged in aftercare. I can only go and do a Bible study for trafficked victims." It's just being willing to think big.

DT: As a mom of eight kids, what type of world do you long for them to live in? Not just five years from now, but 10, 20, 30, 40 years from now.

Stacia: Wow. That's thought provoking. In the context of this issue, I don't want my children to ever be afraid of staring a big issue in the face, and I really want them to be givers. I think we focus a lot on me, me, me and what I can achieve and where I can go and what is success for me. But, I really want my kids to be engaged in how they impact someone else, what it's like to give. Obviously, I want them to be in safe situations and for them to live in a world where we don't have oppression at all and children aren't abused or exploited. I desire that for them.

But, I really desire for them to be part of the solution and not be afraid to engage in things that may not be popular or may not be, you know, accepted or maybe hard topics to dive into, but to be willing to roll their sleeves up and get their hands dirty, because that's really what it takes.

I'm reminded that it's one person at a time, and that if I can just impact one life, one community, then that's worth it. One child that doesn't have to spend another night in a dirty bed servicing someone when they should never have to do that ever no matter how old they are. I'm just reminded that it's just taking small bites of a big problem, and it takes all of us together to really address it.

Through collaboration, as people start to be more willing to collaborate, that we really can end slavery in our lifetime. Over eight years ago when I got involved, when you talked about this issue, people covered their face and closed their eyes and wrote you a check. "I'm going to write you a check and don't ever tell me about this again."

It's encouraging to see people say, "I'm going to write you a check. I'm going to part of a monthly giving campaign. I'm going to continue to write checks, but I'm also going to find out what's going on in my community."

I really believe we can end slavery in this lifetime through partnership and perseverance. Together, we can come together to address meaningful solutions that will ultimately result in ending modern day slavery.

Hope for Justice
Nashville, TN
www.hopeforjustice.org

Hope for Justice identifies and rescues victims, advocates on their behalf, provides restorative care which rebuilds lives and trains frontline professionals to tackle slavery.

31 WAYS to TAKE ACTION

Knowledge without action is of little help to those who are suffering in your city. While not everyone will take up the issue of sex trafficking in America as his or her "cause", we know that many will want (and need) to respond in practical ways. That's why we've assembled a list of possible action steps for individuals, groups, or entire churches/organizations.

PROMOTE AWARENESS & AID PREVENTION

1. **Host a screening of IN PLAIN SIGHT** at your home, school, workplace, or church, and use this Group Study Guide. More info: www.inplainsightfilm.com/screening

2. **Educate yourself, friends, and family** about sex trafficking in the United States by visiting the Polaris Project website for more information – http://bit.ly/USsextrafficking.

3. **Host an information session** and invite a qualified speaker.

4. **Post news stories** about sex trafficking on social media.

5. **Hang posters** with the National Human Trafficking Hotline number (888-3737-888) at motels, restaurants, and restroom stalls. Download the poster at http://bit.ly/sextraffickinghotline.

6. **Form a neighborhood watch group** or educate your homeowners association on what indicators neighbors should be looking for and how to report.

7. **Speak out to local retailers** when they offer products or advertising that glamorize pimping or sexualize children.

END DEMAND

8. **Affirm upstanding men in your community** who exemplify moral conduct and honor women / children with their words and actions.

9. **Discontinue using porn.** If you view pornography, there is a high probability that you will eventually seek to purchase sex. We would encourage you take steps to develop healthy relationships and seek help to recover from this habit / addiction. More info: www.xxx-church.com

10. **Stop purchasing sex.** If you are buying sex, please know that women or children don't enjoy being with you. They fake the experience, because they'll be beaten if they don't bring back enough money or accumulate enough money to support their drug addiction. Please consider getting support and developing healthy relationships through programs like Celebrate Recovery or Sexaholics Anonymous. To find a group in your area, visit www.celebraterecovery.com or www.sa.org.

11. **Mentor young men.** Introduce the "Empowering Young Men to End Sexual Exploitation" curriculum for high school boys at your local schools in order to educate young men about the harms of prostitution and to enlist them as allies in the movement to end violence against women and girls. More info: www.caase.org/prevention

12. **Attend local zoning hearings**, and speak up when someone wants to bring questionable businesses into your community.

ADVOCATE FOR LEGISLATIVE CHANGE

13. **Learn what laws exist** at the city, county, and state levels, and start to understand any deficiencies. Make your voice known to lawmakers, and vote accordingly.

14. **Write or call your local judges and county officials** to encourage them to educate themselves on the issues of sex trafficking, and send them a copy of the IN PLAIN SIGHT documentary.

MAKE A PERSONAL IMPACT

15. **Recognize the signs** that someone may be a victim of sex trafficking – http://bit.ly/signsoftrafficking.

16. **Report suspicious activity** to 911 or the National Human Trafficking Hotline at 888-373-7888.

17. **Invest in the lives of your children** and teaching them that all human beings are to be loved and valued.

18. **Treat women as equal members of society**, and avoid turning women into objects (objectifying) through your thoughts, words, and actions.

19. **Discontinue using the term "prostitute" or "ho"** – understanding that a woman is being prostituted or is prostituting herself. Her identity and value are so much more than being sold for sex.

20. **Discontinue using the term "pimp" or "pimpin" in a positive light** – understanding that there is nothing glamorous or honorable about coercing, manipulating, or forcing a woman to have sex for money.

21. **Give generously** to one of the six non-profits featured in the film that run aftercare homes and fight against sex trafficking – www.inplainsightfilm.com/donate

22. **Dedicate your gift giving** to include products made by survivors or benefitting organizations that are fighting against sex trafficking in the United States. Examples include:
www.penhlenh.com - www.isanctuary.org - www.thistlefarms.org
http://store.nightlightinternational.com

23. **Become a foster parent**, and provide a loving foster home for a child.

HELP YOUR CHURCH MAKE AN IMPACT

24. **Host a prayer event** using an existing prayer guide specifically focused on trafficking. Resources: http://bit.ly/guidetoprayer

25. **Host a fundraiser or benefit concert** for a non-profit that runs an aftercare home and fights against sex trafficking. Recommended organizations: www.hopeforjustice.org

26. **Support educational and vocational programs** in your area for at-risk girls.

27. **Approach your local juvenile justice system** about presenting "Traps of a Trafficker" to female minors on a regular basis. More Info: http://bit.ly/trapsofatrafficker

28. **Start a Celebrate Recovery or support group** for men and women struggling with porn or sex addiction. For more info: www.celebraterecovery.com

29. **Compile a list of counselors in your area** that specialize helping men and women with porn or sex addiction, and have it ready to refer to people as needed.

30. **Host a "Porn and Pancakes" men's event** - a morning filled with straight talk about porn and the issues surrounding porn, from the people who get it. More Info: http://bit.ly/pornandpancakes

31. **Prayerfully consider opening a licensed aftercare home** for survivors of sex trafficking.

WHO TO SUPPORT?

When evaluating aftercare homes to support (beyond the six featured in the IN PLAIN SIGHT documentary), we encourage you to ask these types of questions. Good intentions are not enough. Professionalism and accountability are critical when working with survivors of sex trafficking.

→ Does the program include trauma-informed counseling by a licensed professional?

→ Is the identity of each child/woman kept confidential?

→ Are minors used to fundraise for the organization?

→ Are females and males housed on completely separate properties?

→ Is the facility licensed so there is accountability for policies and procedures?

→ Do those working and volunteering for the facility have to undergo a stringent vetting process?

→ Is the location undisclosed?

THANK YOU

It would be impossible to produce the IN PLAIN SIGHT resources without a dedicated team of talented individuals. Without these men and women, there's no way the documentary, study guide, or album would even exist.

Associate Producers & Donors - without your financial generosity, this project would not be possible. Thank you, thank you, thank you!

Natalie Grant - thank you for investing your time and talent into such an important cause. I admire your dedication and heart for restoration.

Noah Lamberth - your tenacity on this project has been amazing. I can't thank you enough for the countless hours of directing, shooting, and editing.

Troy Lamberth - thank you for your wisdom and keen sense of storytelling that brought out the very best in the film.

Austin Thompson - what an amazing eye you have! Your cinematography and creative editing are deeply appreciated.

David Lamberth - thank you for your hard work, safe driving skills, and willingness to help wherever needed.

Ran Jackson - thank you for creating a beautiful score that engages the viewer. I greatly appreciate your creativity and teamwork.

Dirk Dallas - your work on the motion graphics adds so much to the film, and I am thankful for your investment in the project.

Brodie Alexander - thank you for coloring the film beautifully!

Randy Williams - your willingness to leverage time, talent, and relationships to produce the benefit album is appreciated. You are a good man.

Stacia Freeman - you are awesome. Thank you for being an incredible leader, co-author, and friend.

ABOUT
IN PLAIN SIGHT

IN PLAIN SIGHT is a three-part campaign to help stop sex trafficking in the United States. We are focused on educating the American public on a dark problem that is exploding across the nation and motivating people to take action in their own communities.

IN PLAIN SIGHT: Stories of Hope and Freedom

Executive produced and narrated by Natalie Grant, the documentary features six modern-day abolitionists as they fight sex trafficking across America. Journeying to six US cities, the film opens viewer's eyes to what's happening down the street "in plain sight".

IN PLAIN SIGHT: Devotional and Group Study Guide

After watching the film, individuals and faith-based small groups, Bible studies, and Sunday School classes can use the book to understand and embrace God's heart for the vulnerable and broken in our world.

IN PLAIN SIGHT: Songs of Hope and Freedom

To help fund the work of Hope for Justice, an accompanying music album is available for purchase and features hymns recorded by well-known artists who turn our attention to the hope and healing needed to overcome this darkness. Not only is this an album that can be enjoyed on your own, we hope you'll utilize the songs in a time of weekly worship as you gather with your small group (lyrics included in the back of the devotional/study guide).

Website – www.inplainsightfilm.com
Facebook – www.facebook.com/inplainsightfilm
Twitter – www.twitter.com/inplainsightnow

JOIN THE MOVEMENT

1. HOST A SCREENING

For more information on how to host a screening of the
IN PLAIN SIGHT documentary in your area, go to
www.inplainsightfilm.com/screening.

2. SUPPORT AFTERCARE HOMES

To make a donation directly to one of the
organizations featured in the documentary, go to
www.inplainsightfilm.com/donate.

3. SUPPORT THE FILM

To make a tax-deductible donation to Awaken Media
and help us spread the film across the world, go to
www.storiesoffreedom.com.

www.ingramcontent.com/pod-product-compliance
Lightning Source LLC
Chambersburg PA
CBHW032350280326
41935CB00008B/518